SAVING
animals

Saving Animals

A Future Activist's Guide

Catherine Kelaher

Ashland Creek Press

Saving Animals: A Future Activist's Guide
Catherine Kelaher

Published by Ashland Creek Press
Ashland, Oregon
www.ashlandcreekpress.com

© 2021 Ashland Creek Press
ISBN 978-1-61822-094-3

Library of Congress Cataloging-in-Publication Data

Names: Kelaher, Catherine, author.

Title: Saving animals : a future activist's guide / Catherine Kelaher.

Description: Ashland, Oregon : Ashland Creek Press, [2021] | Audience: Ages 10-21 | Audience: Grades 10-12

Identifiers: LCCN 2020042969 (print) | LCCN 2020042970 (ebook) | ISBN 9781618220943 (paperback) | ISBN 9781618220950 (hardcover) | ISBN 9781618220967 (ebook)

Subjects: LCSH: Animal rights--Juvenile literature. | Human-animal relationships--Juvenile literature.

Classification: LCC HV4708 .K437 2021 (print) | LCC HV4708 (ebook) | DDC

179/.3--dc23

LC record available at https://lccn.loc.gov/2020042969

LC ebook record available at https://lccn.loc.gov/2020042970

This book is dedicated to the animals who are suffering now and the young activists who are striving to help them.

CONTENTS

INTRODUCTION

Congratulations on picking up *Saving Animals: A Future Activist's Guide*. If you're reading this book, I'm guessing you care about animals. Maybe you have recently learned about some of the horrible things people do to animals and it has made you feel angry, frustrated, or sad. Maybe you feel powerless to make a difference, or perhaps you feel shocked by all the new information. Don't worry; these feelings are all normal. Not only that, but here's a secret for you: You can harness the power beneath those negative feelings and turn them into something good—*activism*.

ACTIVISM IS TAKING ACTION WITH THE AIM OF BRINGING ABOUT POSITIVE CHANGE IN SOCIETY. ANIMAL ACTIVISTS KNOW THAT HURTING ANIMALS IS NOT OKAY. WHEN ANIMALS CRY OUT FOR HELP, HUMANS TEND TO IGNORE THEM. THIS MEANS THAT ANIMAL ACTIVISTS MUST SPEAK UP EXTRA LOUD ON THE ANIMALS' BEHALF.

As you read this book, I bet you'll be amazed by the young activists who are featured. Some of them started taking action for animals when they were only a few years old. They saw something they didn't like, and they took action to change it. **Emma Black (14) of Wollongong, Australia**, says, "We may be young, but we're also powerful. People will see us speaking up for animals and will realize that they, too, can make positive changes. Our voices will be heard."

Saving Animals: A Future Activist's Guide is full of inspiration from awesome young activists, as well as activism ideas, animal rights info, and tips on how to care for your activist self. You can either read the book from start to finish, learning about different forms of activism as you go, or you can dip in and out as you please. Here are a few things to expect:

» Activist stories and interviews (if they can do it, so can you!)
» Actions you can take today to make a difference for animals
» How to directly rescue animals

» Step-by-step plans to organize activism events
» Self-care tips for when you feel frazzled from living in a non-vegan world

Who knows where this book will take you? Perhaps you will start an animal rights club in your school, college, or community? Perhaps you will share vegan food with your family and friends? Or maybe you will get out there and rescue some animals. One thing I am sure of is that you will learn that your actions can make a difference. Are you ready to jump in and start saving animals?

Let's go!

Catherine Kelaher
New South Wales, Australia

IF YOU TAKE ACTION FOR ANIMALS AFTER READING THIS BOOK, PLEASE POST A PIC OF YOUR ACTION ON YOUR SOCIALS WITH THE HASHTAG #SAVINGANIMALS. THAT WAY, OTHER ACTIVISTS CAN SEE WHAT YOU'RE UP TO, GET IDEAS, AND GET INSPIRED.

CHAPTER 1

START WITH YOU

You may be surprised to learn that we can spare animals simply by not paying others to hurt them. Every time you or your parents purchase something for you to consume, you are making a statement of what you will and won't accept. If you are not happy that a product causes pain and suffering to animals, one of the most powerful things you can do is refuse to consume it.

What Is "Vegan" (pronounced *vee-gn*)?

Being vegan means you choose not to consume or use products that come from animal use or animal cruelty. It is about reducing the harm we do to animals as far and as practicable as possible. All the activists in this book are happy and healthy vegans.

Why Vegan?

Being vegan is a powerful way to stand up for animals. It's like saying to the industries that abuse animals, "No, you can't have any of my money." Being vegan can cause a ripple effect of kindness when others see how easy, fun, and effective it is. Vegans know that animals are here with us, not for us.

Everyone Is Going Vegan!

As more people learn about animal exploitation, they are choosing to go vegan. As Dan Hancox writes in his article, "The unstoppable rise of veganism: How a fringe movement went mainstream," in *The Guardian*, the number of vegans is soaring, with more and more vegan options becoming available in supermarkets and restaurants. Some vegans choose to leave it at that and simply stop funding cruelty to animals. Others decide to take it a step further and become activists. Let's have a look at some of the ways animals are used in everyday life.

MEET YOUR MEAT

When I was eight years old, my parents took me to a petting zoo. I sat on a straw bale and bottle-fed a lamb. I remember the lamb pulling hard at the rubber teat, and I remember smiling at how adorable this little character was. He had the softest wool, and his tail was wagging back and forth.

That night, my mum cooked lamb for dinner, and as I looked at my plate, I made the connection. The lamb on my plate had been a living, feeling animal with his own personality and desire to live, just like the lamb I had been bottle-feeding. That was the moment I went vegetarian. I didn't want to be part of a system that brings animals into the world just so we can use them and take their lives.

Jacqueline (13) of Ireland, had an interesting way of making the connection between animals and meat. "I read a fictional book called *Eragon* by Christopher Paolini. It's about dragons, but the way he described taking the life of animals; it was horrifying to me. I thought, 'I can't do this anymore.' Shortly after that, my school showed us a video about how chickens are treated before their bodies end up at fast food restaurants. Even the meat eaters were shocked. The chickens were kept in awful conditions, and the way they were killed was horrible."

It's simple, really, isn't it? Meat is made from the flesh of animals. When you find out someone had to die for your meal, you may not find yourself so hungry for meat.

THE PROBLEM OF USE

How do you think you would feel if you were used without your permission? For example, if someone in your class copied your homework without permission and claimed it as their own?

Being used without permission is what happens to animals bred into meat, dairy, and egg farms.

Most commonly, animals are kept in dim, crowded sheds called *factory farms*. In these factories, the animals can hardly move, let alone feel the sun on their skin or the grass beneath their feet. But even if the animals were kept in better conditions, it is still a problem that they are being used. Their bodies are still manipulated by humans, and the individual animals still have their lives ripped away when a human demands it.

Priscilla Huynh (20) of Sydney, Australia, also had an unusual path to becoming vegan. She says, "I was brought up in an Asian household where we ate very unusual things such as pig's ear, pig's blood jelly, and ox tongue. When I was sixteen, I began to think more consciously about what I was eating and realized how gross it was. I stopped eating the more unusual 'foods.'"

Priscilla with rescued hen Ariel

Priscilla continues, "When I was seventeen, my grandma passed away. In Buddhism, after a death, close family and friends eat a vegetarian diet for six weeks. Although my family is not Buddhist, we did it out of respect for my grandma. I had known some of the reasons why people went vegan through watching YouTube videos, but I couldn't fathom just eating plants for the rest of my life."

But then, when she reached the final week, Priscilla says, "I felt pretty good about not eating animals. After all, I had always considered myself an animal lover. I then stumbled across a video by The Vegan Activist called 'Why Vegetarians Should Go Vegan.' It was mind-blowing. I was shocked to learn about how much animal cruelty there was in animal products other than meat. I decided to transition to going vegan from that day."

MEET HOPE

Hope was destined to be one of the chickens you see wrapped in plastic at the supermarket. She had spent the first six weeks of her life on a factory farm, crammed in with lots of other baby chickens. Her body was bred to grow horribly fast so that at six weeks old, while she was still chirping and had baby-blue eyes, she was thrown into a crate to be taken to slaughter. She had been brought into a sad existence by humans who wanted her for her flesh.

That night, a group of kind activists were holding a vigil at the slaughterhouse and asked for a chicken to be released. That chicken was Hope.

"A MAN CAN LIVE AND BE HEALTHY WITHOUT KILLING ANIMALS FOR FOOD; THEREFORE, IF HE EATS MEAT, HE PARTICIPATES IN TAKING ANIMAL LIFE MERELY FOR THE SAKE OF HIS APPETITE. AND TO ACT SO IS IMMORAL." —LEO TOLSTOY

Catherine with rescued hen Hope

I run a chicken rescue in Australia called NSW Hen Rescue, and when my friends from the vigil called me to say they had saved a chicken, I rushed over. I couldn't help crying as I saw her sweet little face.

Once she was safe in my car, I stood by the truck of chickens who were waiting to be killed and tried to send them love, but my heart was breaking.

Back at home, I knew Hope would be scared of humans, so after I made sure she was okay, I gave her a private space where she could feel the sunshine for the first time. I sat down outside on the balcony and said, "Are you okay, Hope?"

Hope cheeped as she walked toward me. She climbed up all the steps to the balcony, hopped onto my lap, and snuggled in. Despite all she had been through, she still wanted human comfort. She wanted love.

Catherine holding vigil for chickens
Photo courtesy of Veronica Rios, Sydney Bird Save

Photo of Oliver Davenport courtesy of Animal Liberation

OLIVER'S STORY

Oliver Davenport (17) of Melbourne, Australia, shares his vegan story.

One of the main reasons I went vegan was because my family friends had a farm. I loved going up there. That was until I was thirteen and I started experiencing what really happens on farms. I witnessed some things that were really screwed up, including castration of lambs and cutting their tails off. That's all standard practice. I saw lambs dying from the cold. In Australia, they breed lambs in winter so they will be ready to slaughter in the spring. They don't have proper shelter. Fifteen million lambs a year die due to the cold.

I watched a video on slaughter. It was meant to be humane, but it was awful. It shut down every excuse I had about farming ethically. The animals are just desperate to live. I never looked back. I made a promise that I would try as hard as possible to make a difference to animals.

Love the taste of meat?

Check out the plant-based alternatives in the supermarket. In most supermarkets today, you can find faux meats by companies such as Tofurkey, Beyond Meat, Gardein, Quorn, and so many more. All delicious and all vegan!

FISHES ARE FRIENDS

Note: In this section, I will use the plural *fishes* instead of *fish* to help portray that these animals are individuals with personalities and relationships.

Fishes are very different from us, but does that mean we should abuse and kill them?

I don't think so.

Fishes are beautiful and intelligent in ways we will never understand. If you read Jonathan Balcombe's book *What a Fish Knows: The Inner Lives of Our Underwater Cousins*, you'll learn just how amazing they are. To our ears, they are silent, but they have other ways of communicating with each other, such as body language and sometimes even clicks and grunts. They cannot scream or grimace when they are hauled out of the water, yet they do feel pain and they do get frightened. As a child, I kept fishes in a tank in my bedroom. The fishes were adopted from my granddad when he got bored with them. A fish tank is not much fun for a fish. At the time, I didn't know better, and I used to love watching the fishes swim and play hide-and-seek in the weeds that we would put in the tank.

My four goldfish were named Fee, Fi, Fo, and Fum, and over the years I got to know their different personalities. Fum was the most boisterous, hiding in the weeds and then jumping out at shy little Fo.

I used to hate it when my dad went fishing. I don't think he felt that comfortable with it either, as when he said he was going fishing, he would usually go to the river to collect litter instead of hurting fishes.

I became even more exposed to the cruelty of fishing when I moved to the beach. I would walk my gorgeous dog, Charlie, by the ocean, and it was heartbreaking to see the anglers haul a fish out of the water and see the poor animal gasping for oxygen. The only good thing was that Charlie loved to pee on the anglers' tackle boxes, and that made me happy.

One day, it was windy and cold, and the beach was empty of anglers. It was wonderful. Charlie and I could run along the edge of the surf, not worrying about tripping over a fishing line or standing on a stray hook. Charlie was extra happy because the wind made him feel energetic.

Halfway along the beach, I saw a sad and familiar sight. There was a large, dead fish left on the sand, with an obvious hole in his lip where the hook had impaled him. I have seen this so many times. Occasionally I would find a fish who was still alive and, after wetting my hands in the water to avoid burning his scales, I would wade into the ocean and release him, hoping he would survive.

I have seen anglers leave a fish gasping for air on the sand, while they stand there trying to catch more. Whenever I see this, I stride over and put the fish back in the water before the fisher can protest. I like this idea from People for the Ethical Treatment of Animals (PETA) to change the dictionary definition of a fisherman:

F is for "fisherman"

noun 1 a person who catches fish for a living or for sport.
or
noun 1 a person ignorant of, oblivious to, or indifferent to the fact that he or she is inflicting pain by catching, suffocating, stabbing, and gutting fish; someone who is hooked on cruelty.

Killing an individual fish is cruel, but commercial fishing is even worse. Fishers use long lines that may be up to a hundred kilometers (or about sixty miles) in length. These lines have hundreds of secondary lines coming off of them, and each line has hundreds of barbed hooks to impale fishes and drag them from the ocean.

Another fishing technique is trawling, which Carl Safina wrote about for Greenpeace (see the For More Information section at the end of this book). A giant, weighted net is slowly dragged along the bottom of the sea, destroying everything and everyone in its path. These nets can be fifty kilometers (about thirty miles) long and can permanently damage ecosystems.

Bycatch is a word for all the animals who are caught when commercial fishers are trying to catch a certain species. For example, for every pound of shrimp caught by trawlers, twenty-six pounds of other animals will be caught and thrown back into the ocean, injured or dead.

These bycatch animals may include other fishes, seahorses, sharks, seabirds, whales, dolphins, manta rays, turtles, and octopuses, to name a few.

Love the taste of fish?

You can get plant-based fish fingers or add a fishy taste to meals by adding healthy and nutritious kelp or dulse flakes.

OCTOPUSES: THE BRAINIACS OF THE OCEANS

Octopuses are known for being super smart, sensitive, and quite mischievous. There have been several stories of octopuses who have used their smarts to escape a life of captivity.

Inky was an octopus who was held captive in a New Zealand aquarium. When his tank lid was left ajar, Inky climbed out of his tank, slid across the aquarium floor, and squeezed down a drainpipe out to sea. A staff member at the aquarium told *The Guardian*, "He is such a curious boy. He would want to know what's happening on the outside. That's just his personality."

(See the For More Information section for a link to the full article.)

There are videos of octopuses escaping slaughter by squeezing through small boat pumps. Aquariums have reported octopuses recognizing members of staff, squirting water at staff members they don't like, disassembling valves to flood the aquarium, and rearranging their tanks the way they want them. Octopuses feel pain and they want to live, so it's sad that they are killed for their flesh.

WHETHER A SEA ANIMAL HAS SUPER BRAINS OR NOT, WE SHOULD RESPECT THEM. LET'S LOOK AT THE OCEANS WITH EXCITED AND RESPECTFUL CURIOSITY AND THINK OF WAYS TO PROTECT THE INDIVIDUALS WHO LIVE THERE.

DAIRY IS SCARY

I still remember the shock and sadness I felt when I found out the truth about dairy. I thought I was making kind choices by being vegetarian, but I still had a lot to learn.

Back in 2005, I was having a fun day out at the Incredible Veggie Roadshow in Wembley, London. I was there with my BFF and fellow veggie, Melissa. We were sampling delicious vegan food, meeting awesome people, and attending informative talks. One of the talks was "The Dark Side of Dairy" by Viva! founder Juliet Gellatley. As she told us the truth about dairy, images flashed up on the screen behind her.

One piece of footage Juliet presented showed a newborn calf being dragged by the leg, away from his mother. The mother looked distraught, pacing and bellowing. They would never see each other again. Every year, the dairy cow goes through the same thing. Again and again, her babies are stolen.

Why are the calves taken away? Well, female mammals can only produce milk after they have given birth. Cows are mammals, so for a female cow to produce milk, a dairy farmer will forcibly impregnate her year after year. Since humans want to use the cow's milk, the calf is not allowed to drink it. Instead, the calves are ripped away from their mothers. Some of the female calves are fed a milk solution and kept until they become adult dairy cows. The other female calves, and all the male calves, are of no use to the industry. They are either killed immediately, sent to saleyards, or raised in veal hutches for a few months before slaughter.

A female dairy cow will suffer painful dehorning and tail-cutting as a calf and four or five years of forced pregnancies, stolen babies, and painful infections of the udder from being bred to produce too much milk. After all that, the cow is worn out. She should live twenty years, but at four or five years old, she is no longer useful to the farmer. She is sent to slaughter. Often, she will be so worn out when she arrives at the slaughterhouse that she will fall to the ground. This is called *downed*. Slaughterhouses are not allowed to sell the meat of downed animals for food, so workers will break the animal's tail, spray her in the face with a hose, pick her up with a tractor, or kick her until she stands. That way the slaughterhouse and farmer can still profit.

After Juliet's talk on dairy, I realized that the dairy industry involves the torture and slaughter of animals. In the photo on the previous page, I am feeding calves named Tuck, Harry, Ingram, Bo, and Maverick. They were born into the dairy industry. These darling boys were rescued by Manning

River Farm Animal Sanctuary and given the love and comfort they always deserved. As I got to know these calves, I felt relief that they were safe, but I also felt sad when I thought of their siblings who were killed and their mothers who remained at the farm, pining for their babies.

Like the taste of dairy?

No worries! There are loads of plant-based milks available, such as soy, coconut, hemp, rice, oat, almond, macadamia, cashew, and more. There's also an abundance of vegan yogurts and cheeses in the supermarket.

EGGSTRA CRUELTY

Eggs are not all they're cracked up to be. Hatcheries breed chicks by the millions to supply people and businesses with hens. The eggs are hatched in incubators and, once hatched, the chicks are put onto a conveyor belt to be sorted into male and female. The girls go on to be painfully debeaked and enter the layer industry, and the boys are killed. Whether you get eggs from caged, barn, free range, organic, or backyard hens, you are supporting an industry that kills male chicks.

DID YOU KNOW?

Hens originate from red jungle fowl who would only lay twelve to thirty eggs a year. Scientists have bred today's laying hens to produce 300–350 eggs a year. This is called *selective breeding* or *genetic manipulation* and is a cruelty that means even hens bought for a backyard still suffer from excessive laying and resulting illnesses like tumors or egg peritonitis.

Egg-laying hens are usually kept in factory farm conditions. Leila (pictured on the previous page) was one of those hens. She had lived her life in a battery farm. She was confined in a cage with six other hens, unable to take more than one step in any direction. She was unable to scratch in the dirt, flap her wings, or feel the sun on her feathers. The photo of Leila was taken the morning after her liberation. It captures the first time she ever saw the sky. Her whole life changed the night before as I gently lifted her from her prison.

Free range and barn living conditions are far from humane. The first time I went to a free range shed, I was amazed that I could not walk across the floor due to the number of hens crammed inside. The girls had to crawl over one another to move. Very few of the hens get to roam outside. If there is an outside area, there is often limited space, very little shelter, and not enough protection from predators.

One of the saddest things is that all hens, whether free range, barn, or caged, will be killed when they are only eighteen months old, due to a decrease in their productivity. Those who are kept in backyards for eggs are often discarded when they stop laying or require veterinary treatment.

At NSW Hen Rescue, I get to meet so many brilliant chickens. It makes me wish everyone could appreciate chickens for the individuals they are. Looking out my window, I will see outgoing Ethel, who welcomes everyone; shy Ariel, who was found almost dead in a battery cage; super friendly Rosemary, who loves to gently preen me; Maddie, who loves cuddles; and Queen Lara, who is scared but gaining confidence every day. She was surrendered when her owner couldn't be bothered to care for her anymore.

We feed the eggs our hens lay back to them; this means the hens can get back some of the nutrients they have lost. Remember, animals are not ours to use. So, when we rescue hens we are asking ourselves what we can do to help the hens, not how we can use them.

Like the taste of eggs?

If you love eggs you can recreate your favorite dishes. Just Google "vegan scrambled tofu" or "vegan hard-boiled egg." You will be amazed at the recipes you find. For baking you can use egg replacer, flaxseed eggs, aquafaba (the juice from cooked or canned chickpeas), or banana or apple sauce, depending on the recipe.

ANIMALS ARE NOT OURS TO WEAR

Some people think clothing such as leather and suede (made from the skins of animals) are by-products of meat, but in truth they are a co-product. They provide the industry with a large amount of income. Animals die so you can use these products, and some are even skinned alive.

Leather and suede are also really bad for the environment. To stop the dead skin rotting, it has to go through a tanning process that involves a lot of chemicals.

Wool is not just a haircut. Shearers are paid by volume and work fast. Deep cuts are a common part of shearing. Some sheep even end up with broken bones from rough handling. As sheep age, the quality of their wool declines, and they get sent to slaughter. Wool requires sheep to be exploited and then to be killed.

Fur is quite literally the stuff of nightmares. I love burying my face into the fur of my cat, Dylan. He is soft and warm. But he reminds me that other animals with beautiful coats suffer every day. Some wild, furry animals are caught in traps that snap shut with immense pressure on their legs or necks. Others are raised in fur farms, where they live in barren, filthy cages. The animals go crazy with boredom and pain until they are killed by electrocution, gassing, or poison. Again, many will be skinned alive.

Silk is made from boiling silkworms alive. Three thousand silkworms die to make every pound of silk.

Pineapple, mushrooms, and cork, oh my!

There are so many other materials we can use instead of animals' bodies, including kind and exciting alternatives. Designers are using fruit and veg skins like apple, pineapple, and mushroom to make soft and fashionable shoes and garments. Some companies are even working on growing leather in a laboratory without using animals. Polyurethane is a synthetic version of leather that is often used by designers.

If you choose to wear these vegan materials, you can buy or make a colorful button that reads *faux*, or even more specific, *pineapple leather*. This may start some conversations about the cool new fabric and why you don't wear animal skins.

ANIMALS ARE NOT OURS TO TEST ON

Let me introduce you to four adorable guinea pigs. From left to right, we have Esther, Elvis, Piper, and Pudding.

They were terrified when I first adopted them. These days they live a happy life, bossing me around and squeaking at me to make sure I give them enough greens. They do happy hops when they are outside and cuddle up to one another at night. They were born in a laboratory, destined to be tested on and killed. Thankfully, a kind lady called Emma started an organization called Research Animal Rehoming Service and was able to rescue these sweethearts, as well as hundreds of other animals.

Despite how outdated it seems, humans still test cosmetics, medicines, and household products on animals. The tests are scary, painful, and nearly always end in the death of the animal. Imagine if someone dripped shampoo in your eyes or forced you to take huge quantities of chemicals to see how much it took to kill you. While rodents, guinea pigs, and rabbits are most commonly tested on, all kinds of animals are used for tests, including dogs, cats, primates, goats, chickens, fishes, and more. However, it's easy to find cruelty-free products. Just look for the words *cruelty free*, *not tested on animals*, or *vegan* on the label. We need to support organizations, like Physicians Committee for Responsible Medicine (PCRM.org), that are campaigning to stop research on animals. They look for cures for diseases without using painful, cruel, and useless animal tests.

SPECIESISM

Speciesism is when someone thinks it's okay to use and abuse animals just because they are from another species. In our society it is very common for someone to be speciesist. Just because it is common does not make it okay. We should always try to challenge speciesism wherever we see it. An example of speciesism is when some dog and cat shelters have meat barbecues to fundraise for their shelters. Why are the pigs, cows, and chickens they are cooking less worthy of care than dogs and cats? The truth is that farmed animals are just as deserving of care, but due to speciesism many people cannot see this.

Single-issue Campaigns

When you speak out about one aspect of animal use (e.g., horse racing), that is called a single-issue campaign. Some people feel that single-issue campaigns are ineffective as they don't usually address the root cause of the problem—that people are speciesist and not yet vegan.

So how can we get around this?

Well, it is important to ensure that a vegan message is behind each of your campaigns. Having veganism as a moral baseline means that going vegan is the minimum you are asking people to do. This way, you can tackle an individual issue and help animals now, while also promoting veganism and sparing more animals of all species in the future.

Live Export

Live export is the commercial transport of animals for slaughter in another country. Animals suffer through grueling trips on overcrowded ships. Many die from heat stress or lack of ventilation during transport. But sometimes when people protest live export they suggest that slaughter in the animals' home country is kinder. In reality, animal slaughter anywhere is painful, unnecessary, and terrifying. So while protesting live export is important, all leaflets and other materials should have a vegan message. The kind alternative to live export should be a vegan lifestyle, not slaughter in another country.

ANIMAL USE IS THE PROBLEM. WE NEED TO REMIND PEOPLE THAT THERE IS NO HUMANE WAY TO SLAUGHTER AN ANIMAL WHO DOESN'T WANT TO DIE.

Horse Racing

When I was about thirteen years old, a friend who also loved horses brought a video around for me and my BFF, Melissa, to watch. It was about horse racing and the cruelty involved. The three of us pony-mad girls were shocked by what we saw.

Why Is Horse Racing Cruel?

I know what you're thinking: How can a fun day out at the races be cruel? You may have seen horses fall in races and get shot for even minor injuries. You may have seen them being whipped relentlessly. You may have seen them bleeding from their nostrils. You may even know that racing horses are often stabled in unnatural, boring conditions. But wastage is far more hidden.

What Is Wastage?

As Mark Russell writes about in his article, "Action urged on killing of 'slow' horses and dogs," in the *Sydney Morning Herald*, wastage is the term for all of the horses who are bred into the racing industry but are "not good enough." Millions of horses worldwide who are bred into the racing industry are slaughtered each year. We aren't just talking about ex-racehorses, either. Even foals who are "not good enough" may find themselves transported long distances to slaughter. And breeding mares (female mother horses) are killed when they are no longer "useful."

So you can see why many animal rights activists are coming together to highlight the cruelty and to bring horse racing to an end. Many of the young activists in this book have attended protests against horse or dog racing (the same killing happens in dog racing). As a single-issue campaign, this may be ineffective, as it is a bit like saying, "It's not okay to race horses, but it is okay to eat cows." How can we expect people to make the connection with racehorses if they still think it's okay to kill other animals? To get around this, you can include vegan messaging on your campaigning websites and leaflets and on your socials in addition to the truth about horse or dog racing. That means you have veganism (kindness to all animals) as your moral baseline.

FOR MORE INFO ON HORSE RACING GO TO: HORSERACINGKILLS.COM.
FOR MORE INFO ON GREYHOUND RACING GO TO: GREYHOUNDCRUELTY.
COM.

HOW TO GO VEGAN

Okay, so you can see why going vegan is a great way to spare animals. But how do you do it? Going vegan is easier than you think. Some people do it overnight. Others may start by going vegan for one day a week or replacing one animal product at a time. Do what suits you best, and soon it will be second nature.

Haile Thomas (19), New York City

Haile Thomas (19) of New York City has helped hundreds of people transition to a vegan diet. She says, "If you are looking to go vegan and don't know where to start, I'd suggest slowly adding more of your favorite fruits and vegetables into your favorite meals as well as swapping out animal products for cruelty-free options. For example, if you have cereal for breakfast, use almond, cashew, or coconut milk instead of cow's milk. For dinner, replace meat with a plant protein like tofu, tempeh, or beans. There are loads of fantastic online resources for delicious recipes. This is a really good way to approach the lifestyle without getting overwhelmed. It's also a good strategy to become exposed to new ingredients and to see plants as an easy replacement for animal products. It is all part of changing your mindset as to what a plate looks like. Approach your meals with fun and curiosity. I began to see plant foods as the start of my plate and not just a measly side dish to every meal."

Being vegan feels great because every day you are making a difference to animals. You are also sending a message to your friends and family that it is fun and effective to be a happy, healthy vegan.

DISCUSS WITH YOUR FRIENDS...

Is it okay for humans to use other animals as we see fit?

If yes or no, discuss why.

CROWD IT OUT

Don't stress about the foods you are cutting out; think of all the delicious plant-based foods you can crowd in and the recipes you can create. Approach it as an adventure and see how many new vegan foods you can try. If you have a favorite meal such as lasagna, simply do a web search for *vegan lasagna* and get ready to try out some recipes.

EASY SWAPS

SWAP THIS	FOR THIS
Meat (flesh)	Vegan hot dogs, veggie burgers, tofu, seitan, textured vegetable protein, jackfruit, beans, legumes
Cow's milk	Soy, almond, cashew, oat, rice milk
Cow's cheese	Plant-based cheese, nutritional yeast, cashew cheese
Eggs to eat	Scrambled tofu, Just Egg
Eggs for baking	Egg replacer powder, flaxseed egg, banana, apple sauce, aquafaba
Leather	Polyurethane, pineapple leather, mushroom leather, cork

The first weeks of being vegan are the hardest because you will be reading labels to look for all those annoying hidden animal ingredients. But remember: This is not about perfection. It's about doing your best for the animals. Soon you will know which supermarket products are accidentally vegan (like Oreos) and which contain milk or eggs.

CHECK OUT VEGANUARY.COM AND SIGN UP AT ANY TIME OF YEAR TO BE GUIDED THROUGH THE FIRST MONTH OF YOUR VEGAN ADVENTURE.

BEING VEGAN MEANS YOU SPARE 198 ANIMALS PER YEAR. IMAGINE IF YOU CAN INFLUENCE OTHERS TO GO VEGAN, TOO. YOU COULD BE A REAL VEGAN HERO!

Charlotte at Jacobs Ridge sanctuary

CHARLOTTE'S VEGAN STORY

Everyone's experience of going vegan is slightly different. **Charlotte Lim (22) of Sydney, Australia**, tells us about how she became vegan. "As a child I never really liked eating meat. I hated the texture of it. Biting into something and getting a mouthful of cartilage, tendon, or skin was never my idea of appetizing!"

"I grew up caring for chickens, and it was my older sister who first made the connection between the animals who we both loved and those on our plate. My sister was the first to stop eating chickens, and then eggs. It made me think about doing it, but I thought. 'Oh, it's too hard. There are so many things that I love eating that I'd miss out on.' A lot of my favorite foods were those linked to my Malaysian-Chinese heritage, and they involved meat and eggs."

Learning About Intersectionality

Feminist Kimberlé Williams Crenshaw coined the term *intersectionality* in 1989. She wrote about the idea that different forms of oppression cannot be isolated. In other words, no one lives in a single category. If you are a woman and a person of color, then those two aspects of your identity will affect how you experience life and how you may experience oppression. If you are differently abled, trans, and a woman then those three aspects of your identity will intersect and affect your life. Like racism, sexism, and ableism, speciesism will affect how someone experiences life. Being exploited and oppressed due to your species is speciesism.

Chickens bred into the meat industry will experience speciesism and ableism, as they are purposefully bred to be so big they are hardly able to walk by the time they are six weeks old.

The intersectionality framework can also be used when looking at issues that oppress multiple groups. For example, if a rainforest is cut down it will affect the environment that is destroyed, the wild animals who are killed and lose their homes, and the indigenous population who also lose their homes.

Charlotte and Kourtney

For Charlotte, learning about intersectionality got her thinking more deeply about animal rights. "Everything clicked when I was in first-year uni. I consider myself a feminist and took gender studies. In one lecture, I learned about the feminist concept of intersectionality. My lecturer who taught me about intersectionality made me question myself and my ethics: If I was a feminist who wouldn't discriminate against someone because of their race, age, or sexuality, why would I continue to contribute to the oppression of an animal, just because of their species?"

Charlotte continues, "For example, due to their biological sex and species, cows are exploited for their female reproductive organs to produce dairy milk. This would not be the case if the species of the animal was different; for example, if the animal was a dog or a cat. Who would drink the milk of a dog or cat? See how bizarre it is? I realized then that something needed to change. In order to live by my feminist values, I had to go vegan. And that was the start of my vegan journey."

Charlotte Makes the Change

I began my transition to a vegan lifestyle while I was on a study abroad program at Lund University in the south of Sweden, very close to Copenhagen. One of the reasons why I chose Sweden was because of how vegan friendly it is. Sweden is a pioneer in terms of vegan alternatives for almost everything—cream cheese, ice cream (the most important thing!), meat and fish, prawns, butter—almost everything I could think of. It was so refreshing being able to experience all the things I thought I'd "miss out" on diet-wise and realize going vegan wouldn't be as much of a challenge as I had expected.

I could still have all the foods from my culture that I loved by eating plant-based replacements, but it did take some courage for me to expand the range of foods I ate. Would you believe I'd never eaten kidney beans before 2019? I'd been alive for twenty-one years and hadn't eaten beans. Neither had I eaten olives. It's astounding and amazing to see how much my diet and palate have expanded since going vegan. Food is one of my greatest pleasures and passions in life, and that's become even better now that I'm vegan.

Making vegan friends on the exchange also helped validate my decision, and they supported me during the periods when I was adjusting.

When I came home from the exchange, my parents disapproved of my veganism, but I'd been vegan for an entire year by the time I moved back in with them, and they were resigned to the fact that I'd made up my mind and it was a final decision. In saying that, going vegan pushed me outside of my comfort zone to expand my social circle to people who *did* share a vegan ethical framework—and the new friendships I've made are so much stronger since we share and appreciate the same values.

If you are going vegan, I would highly recommend getting involved in animal rights. Volunteering at NSW Hen Rescue has reinforced how horrific the egg industry is and has strengthened my conviction to continue advocating for animal rights.

ANIMAL ACTION

What animal rights issues can you think of that intersect with other social justice issues?

For example, racism and classism ensure people in low-income areas live in food deserts and do not have access to healthy, vegan food. This is a problem for the people as they will find it harder to be healthy. It is a problem for animals, too, as it means people who live in these areas will struggle to be vegan, and therefore more animals will be killed.

What other issues can you think of that intersect with each other?

QUIZ – ARE YOU A VEGAN SUPERHERO?

Test your animal rights knowledge before we zoom further into the world of saving animals.

1. At what age are male chicks killed in the egg industry?

    a) 6 weeks old

    b) 18 months old

    c) 1 day old

2. Leather and suede are made from the skin of an animal. Do vegans wear these products?

    a) Yes. Leather is a by-product of the meat industry, so it doesn't hurt animals to wear it.

    b) No, because leather gives vegans a rash.

    c) No, because leather causes harm to animals.

3. Which two answers do you think are true about milk?

    a) Mother cows have to have a baby calf to produce milk.

    b) There are lots of milks available that are made from plants.

    c) Cows would explode if they were not milked.

4. Can a fish feel pain?

    a) No.

b) Yes, but only when the water temperature is below ten degrees.

c) Yes, they feel pain.

5. Do bees get hurt when people farm honey?

a) No, bees make honey for people to eat.

b) No, bees fly away to safety when people come near the hive.

c) Yes, bees make honey for themselves to eat, and some get killed when people collect honey.

6. Being vegan is a way to choose to not contribute to animal exploitation, but can you get enough nutrients being vegan?

a) Yes, no supplements are needed.

b) No, it's not possible.

c) Yes, if you eat fish as well.

d) Yes, if you take a B12 supplement.

7. Hens originate from red jungle fowl who lay twelve to thirty eggs a year, but humans have exploited hens' reproductive systems so now they lay a lot more. How many eggs do laying hens lay a year?

a) 25–50

b) 75–100

c) 300–350

d) 6,000 –7,000

8. No one is perfect, and whatever we do, we hurt some animals, especially little ants with our big old clown feet. What is the point of being vegan, if we can't be perfect?

a) To reduce as much suffering as possible.

b) To get to Level 5 Vegan so you can criticize other people.

c) There is no point.

Turn the page to check your answers.

ANIMAL ACTION

If you're new to veganism, try these challenges:

Supermarket Recon—Go to the local shops and see what vegan food you can find. Can you find any veggie sausages? Veggie burgers? Any vegan chocolate? Any vegan cake mix? Vegan cheese? You can even check your favorite snacks to see if they are "accidentally vegan," meaning they are not labeled as vegan but happen to have no animal products.

Vegan Chef—Write down your five favorite meals. Your challenge over the next month is to veganize them! Search Google or YouTube to help you. Whatever you want to make, you can be pretty sure another vegan has already done it.

ANSWERS

1. **C.** I know it's shocking, but male chicks are killed at only a day old in the egg industry. If you got this right, you get **3 points.**

2. **C.** You may have heard that leather is just a by-product. The truth is, the skin is the most valuable part of a cow's body. Even without meat there could be a trade of cows' and lambs' skin, so it is important to boycott this industry to save animals. If you got this right, you get **3 points.**

3. **A and B**. Cows must have a calf to produce milk. The calf is then taken away from his mother, which is scary and sad for both mum and baby. It is totally unnecessary when we have so much plant-based milk to choose from. If you got this right, you get **3 points.**

4. **C.** Yup, fishes feel pain, all right. Imagine having a hook stuck through your lip. Ouch! If you got this right, you get **3 points.**

5. **C.** Yes, some of the bees get killed when farmers take their honey. Farmers sometimes cut the wings off queen bees, and as worker bees are so loyal they will not leave her even if there is danger. Honey farmers kill whole hives during certain times of the year. Honey is a food that bees work hard to make for themselves. Let's be kind to bees. If you got this right, you get **3 points.**

6. **D**. You sure can be healthy on a vegan diet. If you eat plenty of vegan food you should get enough protein, vitamins, and minerals. The only thing you will need to supplement is vitamin B12. B12 is only made by bacteria. It used to occur naturally in the soil, but now the soil is depleted of B12. The reason B12 is in meat is because farmers inject animals with it. Cut out the middleman and take some B12 tablets yourself. They only cost a few dollars and are available at pharmacies and supermarkets. If you got this right, you get **3 points.**

7. **E**. Scientists and farmers have selectively bred hens to lay 300–350 eggs per year. How greedy and cruel. This means that hens suffer tumors and other health problems as they age. Whether hens are caged, free range, or in the backyard, they are suffering from over-laying. If you got this right, you get **3 points.**

8. **A**. No one is perfect, but that doesn't mean we should do nothing at all. Don't be too hard on yourself. If you got this right, you get **3 points.**

Now tally up your points!

Score 18–24 — Vegan Superhero

It's time to put on your mask and practice swishing your cape. You know your stuff. I'm guessing you've been doing some research about how animals suffer when humans use them. The main thing is to keep learning and put your knowledge into action by living as kindly as possible. You may already be doing some activism, but after learning about what happens to animals, you are desperate to do more. Use this book for more vegan inspiration, and be sure to check out the chapter on self-care if you feel overwhelmed.

Score 9–17 — Vegan Sidekick

You know a fair bit about animal rights. You may have heard some animal rights stories in the news or seen the odd vegan video that has popped up in your socials. You may feel sad about some of the things you've seen and wonder what you can do about it. Don't worry; there's plenty you can do. Start by doing more research via the resources on the next page so you really know your stuff, and read on to find out how to turn your new knowledge into action.

Score 0–8 — Vegan Squad

When you see someone being cruel to an animal it makes your blood boil. But you haven't been exposed to many animal issues just yet. You may understand why eating meat sucks, but the cruelty involved in milk, eggs, dairy, and entertainment may be new to you. That's okay! We all have to start somewhere. Check out some of the great resources below to learn more and educate yourself so that you are in an even better position to help animals. You can start helping animals right now by stopping contributing to their suffering. Woo-hoo! The animals are gaining another friend.

CHECK THESE OUT

LoveAllAnimals.com.au

Veganuary.com

SOS.PETA.org

YouTube.com/user/BiteSizeVegan

CHAPTER 2

FAMILY MATTERS

Now that you know the truth about how animals are used, you probably want to shout it from the rooftops. It's normal to hope that when your friends and family find out what you know, they will all go vegan, too. I mean, they are pretty great people, so why wouldn't they feel the same way you do?

We want our loved ones to understand and care about animal exploitation as much as we do, but they can often be the very hardest people to convince. Trust me, I'm speaking from experience here. I love my brother, but we have to avoid the topic of animal use; otherwise, I get angry and he gets stubborn.

It's even harder when you are young and living at home. You may rely on your guardians to buy your food. Maybe your mum or dad usually makes your dinner. Hopefully these handy hints from some amazing young vegans can make things easier for you.

Charlotte Lim (22), Sydney, Australia: "Apart from my older sister, my family was definitely not supportive of my decision to go vegan. Although I'd spoken to my family about being vegan before, the reaction of disapproval was so strong from my parents that at first, I dealt with it by going vegan in secret. Over time I realized I needed to be truthful about my veganism. My parents saw how much happier I was, and that helped them warm to the idea and become more accepting. I also introduced them to vegan documentaries and new recipes and foods, which helped them respect my decision."

Emma Black (14), Wollongong, Australia: "It was a difficult path trying to get my parents to allow me to be vegan, but I stood my ground and refused to eat eggs or dairy. I did loads of research and watched numerous documentaries. That got me questioning my family's lifestyle choices. Within a month of me going vegan, my mum became vegan as well. My brother is currently vegetarian, and my dad is well on his way to being vegan. One of the ways I got through to my family was by cooking for them. I cook about five to six days a week. I just love cooking. For dinners I try to veganize traditional recipes that my family loves, like tacos, pizza, and sushi. I try to replicate the original taste. I love baking as well and have even done some vegan bake sales. I don't use recipes; I just look in my fridge and see what I have there. I put everything onto my bench and create something. Delicious food is a great way to get people interested in veganism and show that you can have a healthy, nutritious diet as a vegan."

Hannah McKay (16), Orange, New South Wales, Australia: "My mum grew up on a cattle farm, so she wasn't particularly open to me being vegan. Even when I went vegetarian, Mum was worried I wasn't getting enough iron, calcium, or protein. She thought I was going to die. I tried to explain that sesame seeds and leafy greens have loads of calcium, but she didn't understand. It's been a work in progress, but now she sees I am happy and healthy, she is much more understanding. I suggest doing as much research as possible. Have all your facts and resources ready to back you up."

Haile Thomas (19), New York City: "If you are having trouble convincing your family to support you in your veganism, then it is best to get educated about the many benefits of veganism together. Watch documentaries, read books, research nutrients and supplements. Try different and new products, and visit vegan restaurants as a fun family adventure. Understanding the ins and outs of a vegan lifestyle is very important in order for your family to adapt to the change."

Kevin Courtney Black (22), California: "When my family found out I was going vegan, they were in disbelief. They told me it wasn't going to last. At the time I was 210 pounds and was beginning to slip into my family's predetermined idea that I was going to be obese. My mom did sort of support me, but she told me I should've stayed vegetarian. The lack of support wasn't too damaging to me as I was prepared for it. My family has never been big on fruits and vegetables. Now I am 152 pounds, and my mom is vegan, too. If you want to go vegan, do your research. The more you research, the more you will feel confident and be able to inform your family. YouTube can be so helpful if you watch those "What I Eat in a Week" videos. It's also helpful to research vitamins you can benefit from taking as a vegan. For example, I only take vitamin B12 as I get other vitamins and nutrients in my diet every day. I had an advantage as I met with a registered dietician to help sort out my intake of nutrients."

Katie Lynch-Dombroski (17), Denver, Colorado: "My parents took some convincing. Mum was fine when I went pescatarian; in fact, she did it with me. But when I realized how unsustainable fishing was and I went vegan, she was concerned about me getting enough nutrients. It was a matter of teaching my family how to adapt. I researched into protein, vitamins, and minerals. I liked cooking and baking anyway, so I enjoyed finding recipes and veganizing them. I found substitutes and vegan recipes on YouTube."

Bailey Mason (16), Sydney, Australia: "When I told my mum, 'No, I don't want to eat animals,' I was sobbing and crying. I was so upset by footage I had seen of so-called 'humane' slaughter of pigs. There was nothing humane about it. Mum initially didn't think I would stick to my vegan lifestyle, but I made it clear that I was very passionate about it. It's really good now because Mum is fine with it. In fact, she is vegan, too. Her mindset changed after seeing the footage."

Jasmine Shaw (18), Central Coast, Australia: "My family doesn't seem to understand my veganism. I don't always bring it up with them as they get very defensive, and when I do talk about it we often end up having a big argument. Mum was worried about my nutrition at first, and she watched everything I ate. Now she knows I am serious about this. Whilst she doesn't love that I'm vegan, she sometimes makes me vegan options and we eat it together. Things have definitely got better over time."

TO SUM UP ...

» Do your research and be prepared for your family's questions.
» Cook and bake vegan versions of your family favorites.
» Take a B12 supplement.
» Watch vegan documentaries or read vegan books with your family.
» Stick to it and show them that this is not a fad.

ANIMAL ACTION

1. Make vegan cookies for your brothers, sisters, or friends.

2. Talk about animals with your family. Ask if you can watch an animal-friendly movie together or some Bite Size Vegan videos on YouTube.

QUESTIONS AND ANSWERS

When you go vegan, you will probably get asked a whole lot of questions. Your family may have concerns about whether you are getting enough nutrients. School friends may try and trip you up with hypothetical questions. If you start doing some vegan outreach, then members of the public may have a lot of genuine questions. Let's take a look at some of the common questions and concerns people may have and how you can answer them.

IF PEOPLE HAVE GENUINE QUESTIONS, TRY TO LISTEN TO THEIR CONCERNS AND STAY CALM AS YOU RESPOND. IT MAY BE THE 100TH TIME YOU HAVE BEEN ASKED, "WHERE DO YOU GET YOUR PROTEIN?" BUT IT MAY BE THE VERY FIRST TIME THE ASKER HAS THOUGHT OF IT.

So, where do you get your protein?

Some people believe that only meat contains protein. WRONG! Plants have protein, too. Do you know who aren't protein deficient? Cows. And they only eat grass (but don't worry, you won't have to do that). Rhinos are also herbivores, and take a look at the muscles on them. Here are some high-protein vegan foods: beans, legumes, nuts, seeds, lentils, tofu, tempeh, plant-based meats (such as vegan hot dogs, seitan, and nut meat), peanut butter, soy milk, protein shakes, and hummus. Even a cup of cooked spinach has five grams of protein. If your parents are still worried about protein, tell them about some of the awesome plant-based athletes who are strong and healthy on a vegan diet. Watch the documentary *The Game Changers* about plant-based athletes.

Where do you get your iron?

Iron is essential to help red blood cells carry oxygen around the body. Iron deficiency is the most common nutrient deficiency in North America. Luckily, it is not hard for vegans to get plenty of iron. Iron is available in beans, grains, nuts and seeds, tempeh, tofu, legumes, Swiss chard, and tomato sauce, to name a few.

DID YOU KNOW?

It's not just about how much iron you consume but also about how easy it is for the body to absorb. By eating vitamin C–rich foods and iron-rich foods together, you can increase your iron uptake five times. This happens naturally in lots of meals. For example, iron in beans combined with vitamin C in salsa can make vegan nachos a super healthy meal. If your parents are anxious about iron, let them know that investing in a cast-iron skillet to cook with will increase the iron content of your meals.

Where do you get your calcium?

Many plant-based milks are fortified with calcium, but there are plenty of other vegan calcium sources, such as chia seeds, almonds, sesame seeds, beans, broccoli, blackcurrants, and figs, to name a few.

Do vegans need supplements?

Yes, it is important that vegans take a vitamin B12 supplement. B12 is naturally produced by bacteria and many years ago would have been found in the soil and consumed when people ate veggies. The soil used in agriculture is now depleted of vitamins and minerals, so vitamin B12 deficiency is common in a lot of people, not just vegans. To ensure the general population gets B12, farmed animals are given B12 supplements by the farmer. By taking a vitamin directly, we vegans are just cutting out the middleperson.

TELL YOUR PARENTS: COUNTRIES THAT CONSUME THE LEAST DAIRY HAVE THE LOWEST RATES OF OSTEOPOROSIS. (CHECK OUT THE FOR MORE INFORMATION SECTION AT THE END OF THIS BOOK FOR DETAILS.)

Where do vegans find recipes or foods?

Spend some time online with your friends or family searching for the vegan versions of your favorite recipes. Just as with non-vegan versions, you can find a huge range of recipes, from easy to complex, from cheap to expensive. Choose recipes that suit your budget, time availability, and skill set. Finding the vegan products at the supermarket may involve a bit of label reading at first, but you only need to do it once to know what is vegan and what is not. If you need a bit of help, just ask in your local vegan Facebook group. Some meals can be super simple, such as using plant milk on your usual cereal, or having hummus, tabbouleh, and falafel for lunch.

We have canine teeth for a reason.

It's true, we have canine teeth, although compared to the teeth of a carnivore, like a lion, ours look like blunt, little stubs. Even if we did have lion teeth, it doesn't give us an excuse to use and abuse animals when we can live happily and healthily eating plants.

Plants feel pain.

It's amazing how often people become plant-rights activists when faced with a vegan. First things first: These people probably eat plants as well as meat. They are not so much concerned about plants as trying to trip you up. Plants do not have a brain or a central nervous system, and they are not sentient. It wouldn't make sense for them to feel pain because, unlike animals, they cannot move away from the source of the pain. But for the sake of this argument, let's assume plants do feel pain. Well, farmed animals are fed far more plants than human vegans could ever eat. So by eating meat, you are contributing to the death of both plants *and* animals. If you really care about the feelings of plants, you need to eat them directly.

Lions are part of nature and they eat meat.

They sure do. Does that mean that we have to, too? I mean, lions also poop outside. Do we have to do that, too? Lions would eat humans if given half a chance. Do we have to do that, too? Let lions do their thing, and we'll do ours.

But you step on ants …

Sadly, it's true. Everyone harms animals in everyday life, even if we don't mean to. We may accidentally step on bugs. Medications may have gone through ineffective animal experiments. There may be animal products in the roads we walk on or the money we handle and spend. The thing is, we will never be perfect, but that is not an excuse to be mean. We can do as much as we can to reduce the harm we cause. As the world becomes kinder and more people are vegan, there will be fewer animal products, so alternatives will be used.

Animals are killed for your vegan food, too.

Unfortunately, current farming practices mean that animals are killed during harvesting of plants. Insects, mice, and other animals get caught up in the harvesting process. This is really sad, and I hope one day technology will exist to reduce this harm. In the meantime, vegans aim to cause as little harm as possible. People who eat meat are causing the death of the same animals to produce the grain to feed the animals they are eating. They are also causing the suffering and death of the animals they are eating.

This is your personal choice. Respect my personal choice to eat meat.

A personal choice shouldn't have a victim. A true personal choice could be what kind of activism you do, what shirt you wear, what color you dye your hair. A personal choice should not be who dies for your dinner. That is a choice that affects others. That is why a lot of vegans feel they want to do more to help animals than just being vegan. When they find out about the horrible things happening to animals, they want to take action to show other people why being vegan is so important.

One person can't make a difference.

Just because one person may not be able to make everything right for animals does not mean that we should do nothing at all. The fact is, one person really *can* make a difference. Just have a look at some of the activism the young people in this book are doing. Wow!

You think you're better than everyone else.

Being vegan doesn't mean someone thinks they're better than anyone else. Vegans do not want to lord power over animals or humans.

If you were on a desert island and there was only a pig to eat, what would you do?

Vegans get this question a lot. It relates to the mythical island where all new vegans find themselves with only a pig for company. **Charlotte Lim (22) of Sydney, Australia**, says, "I would make friends with the pig. But if I was pushed to answer in more detail, I'd argue from a logical point of view. There are just so many inconsistencies and other factors that would have to be taken into account in this hypothetical question. I would look for plants to eat. Maybe kelp? And I would try to find something for the pig to eat, too."

So while this question is hypothetical, people are trying to test your ethics. I like to say, "What is the pig eating? I'll eat that."

This is just a phase.

Family may try to minimize your choice to be vegan by calling it a phase or a fad. The way to prove this is important to you is to do your research and to stick with veganism. In a year's time, when you are a happy vegan, you will have shown them this is not a fad.

Photo courtesy of Charlize Reynierse

If you go vegan, all the cows will go extinct.

The idea that we should breed animals into existence just to be enslaved by us is quite sickening. If you look at an animal in a factory farm or being slaughtered after life at a family farm, I think you would agree that it would be better for the animal never to have been born at all than to experience enslavement and suffering. In a vegan world, there would likely be some cows in sanctuaries. Perhaps we could even rehabilitate extinct, wild cow breeds that were either entirely domesticated or hunted to extinction.

If you go vegan, cows will take over the world.

Non-vegans can get a bit confused here. In a vegan world, would cows be extinct or would they take over the world? The only reason there are so many farmed animals right now is because humans have bred massive numbers of them to use and eat. If we had a vegan world, we would not be breeding these animals into existence. As much as I wish it would, the world will not go vegan overnight. The change will come slowly. If by some miracle we did get a vegan world overnight, then I'm pretty sure all those fab new vegans would come together to find a solution for the animals saved from farms.

Don't you care about people?

Caring about animals and avoiding harming them does not take away from a vegan's ability to care for people. Luckily for us, humans have unlimited compassion to go around. Some awesome vegan people are doing great things for humans. There are vegan food trucks to feed homeless people, fair-trade vegan food companies, and doctors helping people reverse heart disease with a plant-based diet. Also, animal agriculture is a major cause of climate disaster. The industry is responsible for massive water usage, fossil fuel use, deforestation, and water pollution. Veganism is the only way we can preserve the world for future generations. Surely that counts as caring for people?

Suggest to your friends and family watching the documentary "Cowspiracy," which shows the environmental impact of animal industries.

You are not allowed to be vegan.

This can be really tough, especially if you are young and are not in control of the groceries brought into your house. Be kind to yourself. Keep doing your research and presenting it to your parents. Stick to your morals where you can, but if non-vegan food is the only food available to you, do whatever else you can, in your life, to save animals. There will be a day when you'll be old enough to make your own decisions on food. In the meantime, start cooking and preparing some vegan meals for yourself or your family.

What will you eat?

Being vegan is not just about cutting things out. It's about crowding things in and challenging yourself to try new and exciting food. Check out the recipe sites on the next page for some good ideas, but don't stop there. Not sure how to make a vegan lasagna or cupcakes? No worries!

Just do a Google or YouTube search, and you'll have hundreds of recipes to choose from.

Here are some recipe sites to get you started...

OneGreenPlanet.org/channel/vegan-recipe

JLGoesVegan.com/jlrecipes

HaileVThomas.com/recipes

TheKoreanVegan.com

ThePPK.com

TheFullHelping.com

SweetPotatoSoul.com

BOSH.tv

VeganYackAttack.com

FindingVegan.com

PlantBasedOnABudget.com

CHAPTER 3

FINDING YOUR SQUAD

When it comes to staying vegan, community is so important. If you're lucky enough to have friends or family going vegan at the same time as you, then that's awesome. But if you are going at it alone, you will benefit greatly from connecting with a group of like-minded people. Together, you can answer questions, offer support, and motivate one another. It's great to know that others have been through what you are going through, and they can save you some of the learning curve.

There are two options:

» Find an existing vegan community
» Start your own vegan community

Check Facebook and Meetup.com to see if there is a vegan or animal rights group in your area. If necessary, you could ask an adult friend or relative to take you along. You can also join a challenge such as Veganuary.com, where there will be many people going through the same change as you.

If there is nothing in your area, why not start a group? You may find you are soon inundated with people wanting to join. Community is just as important when you decide you want to step up and do even more to help animals. Fellow activists can guide you, inspire you, and support you.

Ateret Goldman (16) of Berkeley, California, is an organizer for Direct Action Everywhere (DxE). She says, "We need community backing this movement. This is something that has been shown across so many successful social justice movements. When you have a community of people who genuinely support each other, it fills you up. It keeps you going. We all have times when we are tired, burnt out, and think of giving up, but when you have community support and a big vision, it keeps you going."

Charlotte Lim (22) of Sydney, Australia, says, "Community has been vital in my own journey in veganism and animal rights activism. Being surrounded by people who share similar values is empowering. Being able to share experiences of a protest or eating at a new vegan café together are some of my fondest memories of being involved with other vegans. Volunteering at NSW Hen Rescue has made the biggest difference. I've been able to learn so much from working with other vegans. We motivate one another, and being surrounded by vegans helps keep me accountable and committed to being vegan."

Priscilla Huynh (20) of Sydney, Australia, says, "I believe it is important to make friends with other animal rights activists as they share your core values and beliefs and will support you and lift you up. If there are no animal rights activism groups near you, set one up yourself. I founded the University of Wollongong's Vegan Society (UOW Vegsoc) in my first year at uni. I am a very introverted person who would get hot flushes and start sweating when I put my hand up in class. If I can do it, I have no doubt that you can, too. We ran events such as the cupcake challenge, potluck game nights where we all brought a dish to share and played games, screenings of vegan documentaries like *Dominion, Cowspiracy,* and *What the Health,* and we even did some video activism as a group."

Priscilla adds, "It is important to have a balance of social events as well as activism events to prevent burnout and encourage others to join the club and get into activism. I was extremely nervous when I first started the club, and I still get nervous speaking at events. You don't have to be the most confident and knowledgeable activist in your community to start a group. I was surprised at how many people were interested in joining the club and wanted to get active but didn't know how or where. I didn't know how to run a club when I first started UOW Vegsoc. The other people that came to the first meeting helped pitch in ideas, and we collaborated. You would be surprised at how many people would like to join; they just need a catalyst. *You can be the catalyst.* The UOW Vegan Society brought together the

Wollongong vegan community and helped some students become vegan and some students become animal rights activists. Some members even went on to organize activism events outside of the university.

"The ripple effect is so powerful, and it stemmed from one person."

Wollongong Vegan Potluck

ANIMAL ACTION

Search Facebook to see if you can find a local animal rights or vegan group in your area. No luck? You can also check Meetup.com and search Google, e.g., "San Diego animal rights club" or "Portland vegan group."

Once you have your online group sorted, it's time to get your group sorted in real life. There may already be an animal rights or vegan club at your school, in which case, join up. Otherwise, you can start your own club. With a kick-ass team behind you …

… you'll be more effective for the animals.

… you will make friends who have similar interests to you.

HOW TO START AN ANIMAL RIGHTS CLUB

Setting up a school or college club is well worth the effort. Start by asking for permission to use a classroom or other space in the school or college for your first meeting. In the rare case that the campus does not allow this, you can always use a team member's house or hold secret squirrel meetings in the playground or a nearby park. Come up with a name for your club so that it's easy to refer to. In my novel *Amanda the Teen Activist*, they called their club "Activist Squad."

Next, make posters to put around the campus advertising your club and letting people know when the first meeting will be. If you can get permission, making an announcement in assembly is a great way to get the word out.

You can use social media to create an online presence for the club and to send out event invites.

Try to be inclusive, and don't say no to anyone who genuinely wants to join the group. Even if someone is not yet vegan, they may be on their way there and can contribute skills and enthusiasm.

Bring some vegan treats and some drinks to the meeting. It's a great ice breaker to get everyone snacking on cruelty-free goodies. Plus, it's a positive way to promote veganism to people who have not yet tried it.

Write a list of any issues you'd like to talk about in your first meeting. Having an agenda will help keep the meeting on track. For your first meeting, you can tell everyone what the goal of the group is and ask if anyone has ideas on what they'd like to talk about. It doesn't have to be a long meeting.

Finishing up by agreeing to an action plan means that things went really well.

Decide on how often you will meet up, and soon you will be unstoppable. Just like that, you have an animal rights team and your voice for animals grew louder.

TIP: FIND OUT WHAT SKILLS EACH MEMBER OF THE GROUP HAS. IS SOMEONE REALLY GOOD AT DRAWING? IS SOMEONE A GOOD WRITER? DOES SOMEONE HAVE A CONTACT IN THE MEDIA? IS SOMEONE GOOD ON THE COMPUTER?

USING PEOPLE'S SKILLS MEANS THAT YOU ARE GIVING EVERYONE A CHANCE TO BE THEIR BEST ACTIVIST SELF. DON'T PUSH ANYONE INTO SOMETHING THEY ARE NOT COMFORTABLE WITH.

THINGS TO DO WITH YOUR ACTIVIST GROUP

Once you have people to work with, there really is no limit to the number of things you can do to help animals. Have a flick through this book and choose an idea to work on as a group. Remember to make veganism the moral baseline.

To start with, you can look for issues going on at your school and see if there are ways you can work to save animals or campaign to make things better.

Not every meeting has to be a problem-solving mission, though. Here are some other things you can do. Some of these activities are just about kicking back with your team.

» Have a vegan pizza night: Watch a fun film (or a vegan documentary) and make vegan pizza.
» Organize a fundraising vegan bake sale.
» Work on an animal rights presentation and get permission to show it to your classmates in assembly.
» Brainstorm ways to use your academic projects to help animals or people.
» Take group trips to animal sanctuaries or vegan cafés.
» Have vegan sleepovers.
» Collect litter at your local creek or beach.
» Leaflet or table in the school corridor.
» Make and put up animal rights posters.
» Make message-wear such as buttons and stickers, and paint vegan messages on blank shirts.

ACTIVIST PROFILE

Katie Lynch–Dombroski (17), Denver, Colorado

One young activist who has taken the idea of a school club and run with it is Katie Lynch-Dombroski of Denver, Colorado. This awesome seventeen-year-old started a vegan food club at her school called Plant-Based Creations. Katie says, "Civil rights are changed socially, and through food activism you can make a difference."

Katie has always loved cooking and baking, so when she went vegan she got stuck into recipes galore. Not only was this fun, but it also helped convince her parents that she could eat a wide range of healthy food without harming animals.

How did the vegan food club start?

It all started on my sixteenth birthday. I invited a load of friends to cook vegan food together at my house. It was so much fun. We made zucchini noodles. My friends all helped, and I realized how much fun it is to cook with other people.

After that I spoke to my culinary teacher and asked if we could use the kitchen labs at school to hold a vegan food club. She liked the idea, and so it began. Now Plant-Based Creations meets every two weeks to cook together.

I'm not the first person to do this, but that's the thing; you don't have to invent something new to change the world.

So how does the club work?

The club is a gathering of anyone who wants to cook vegan food. You don't have to be vegan to come along. It's open to anyone. That's what makes it activism and not just a vegan group. We decide what recipe to make before we meet. We have a spreadsheet, which lists all the ingredients we need. Each person puts their name next to one ingredient and brings that along. At the club, each person takes charge of making one part of the recipe.

We cook together, and then we eat together. It's a great social thing, and it exposes people to delicious vegan food. It is a form of passive activism.

What is passive activism?

It is about making veganism fun and approachable, not some big, scary thing. When I first went vegan, I tried more active forms of activism like leafleting. I found that people didn't respond so well to the gruesome photos, and I felt, for me, it wasn't the most effective way to advocate.

With the food club, we encourage anyone, vegan or not, to come along and cook and enjoy vegan food. They get to have fun and learn that vegan food can be delicious and tasty. Maybe they will cook those recipes for other people in their family. It plants a seed, so if someone talks to them about veganism in the future they have already had a positive experience.

How would you suggest someone start out with food activism?

I started by baking vegan cookies for my friends and teacher at the end of the school year. I wrapped them individually and attached the recipe to each one. I gave them out, and people reacted so well.

If you can get people to try vegan food and see how delicious and familiar it can be, that's a good start. I also bring vegan brownies into the rec center that I work at, and that goes down a treat.

Another good thing to do is a vegan bake sale to raise money for an animal charity.

Plant-Based Creations Club
Learn to cook, bake, and create food using plant-based ingredients!

- Meets every 2nd & 4th Thursday of the month 3:15-4:20

- Located in C101 (by latte bar in west atrium)

- Counts for **CAS!**

Like our Facebook page @LHSPlantBasedCreations!

Tips for your Vegan Food Club Facebook page

Katie says to keep it positive. This is a food page, but you can post infographics every now and then to let people know what is going on with animals and the environment. Katie shares simple recipes and aims to show that vegan food is simple and delicious. Be kind to the people who come to your group. Remember, veganism isn't about being perfect. Practice what you can to minimize negative impacts to animals and the environment, and if you ever mess up, don't beat yourself up. Be kind to yourself and others.

How to Start a Vegan Food Club

1. Find a teacher or parent who is willing to help.
2. Get permission to use school kitchen facilities or see if your parents would let you use theirs.
3. Survey your friends. Ask them if they will help and if they would like to come along. You only need a couple of people to start, and they don't have to be vegan.
4. Set a date for your first meeting and choose a recipe.
5. Make a flyer (like Katie's, on the previous page) that says when and where the meeting will be held, and post it around campus.
6. (Optional) Start a Facebook page where you can post yummy vegan recipes and keep the group updated. Add friends and ask them to add their friends.
7. Make sure everyone knows which ingredient they will bring to the first meeting.
8. Get cooking and enjoy!

VEGAN DATING

Is your crush vegan? It can be tough when you are totally into someone, but they are contributing to the way animals are used and hurt in our society. You like them a lot, but you don't like what they are doing.

So, are you meant to say no when the cutest person you know asks you out—because they are still non-vegan?

First of all, realize that we don't yet live in a vegan world. While it is totally cool if you want to surround yourself with vegan friends, the truth is, it's likely you will have non-vegan friends, too. This actually gives you a great opportunity. When you hang out with non-vegans, you can inspire them with your amazing vegan food, and you can lead by example. You can show that you are a happy, healthy vegan. You may also have more influence to get them to watch a documentary and have a vegan pizza night.

If your date is really interested in you, then they will probably agree to eat vegan on your date. If they start asking loads of annoying questions, you can refer to the questions and answers in the previous chapter for help—but if you've already answered them and they keep going on, maybe they are not as nice as you thought they were?

Hopefully you will have loads of other stuff in common to chat about.

Don't feel like everything you do with your friends has to be about veganism. Go to the movies, go to a party or play a sport, and just have fun. It's a good way to cheer yourself up when you're feeling down.

My husband wasn't vegan when I met him, but after a year or so of dating he went vegetarian and then later vegan. I had so many leaflets and videos about animal rights around the house, he couldn't avoid it. Plus it's one of my favorite topics to talk about.

Some people feel that they just can't deal with their friends consuming animal flesh and secretions. If you have an animal rights team sorted, then perhaps your crush will eventually join. Compassion is pretty hot, after all.

If you don't feel comfortable dating non-vegans, then that's okay, too. Just do whatever feels right for you.

CHAPTER 4

KICKING ASS FOR ANIMALS AT SCHOOL

You may feel that your activism and your studying are constantly battling for time. But there are times when you can combine speaking up for animals with projects you have to complete for school. Just take a look at some of this young activist inspiration.

Caylin King (17), Newcastle, Australia: "When the teacher asked us to create a presentation on a man-made disaster, I thought about factory farming straightaway. It truly is a disaster for people, the environment, and the animals. I used some images from inside factory farms. It wasn't graphic, but people in the class gasped when I told them the facts. It got a strong reaction and was the perfect chance to use the school environment to the animals' advantage. I've also written an essay on the cruelty of dairy and use every chance I get to talk about animals and share their stories at school."

Emi Pizarro Zamora (9), Brisbane, Australia: "Last year I took a pamphlet to school about what happens in slaughterhouses and why being vegan is healthy. I gave my teacher the leaflet. He read it and seemed to understand my veganism better after that. One day at school everyone was going to make milkshakes. I told my teacher, 'I'm sorry, I don't want to drink cow's milk, because I'm vegan.' He said he would make me something else. I brought in a leaflet about milk and he understood. Now he is vegan."

Emma Black (14) of Wollongong, Australia, pictured above, presented a talk on the truth about the dairy industry to her class. The talk was called "Life as a Dairy Cow," and through the story of one cow, Emma shared the realities of what happens in the dairy industry. This was a fantastic opportunity, as most of her class and their parents were not aware of how much cruelty goes on in the dairy industry. And they certainly didn't know about baby calves being taken from their mothers. Not only did Emma reach this class, but she also filmed the talk and published it on YouTube and her socials. This enabled her to reach an even wider audience with her message. She captioned the video with resources to help people become informed on all aspects of veganism.

There are loads of opportunities to speak up for animals as part of your school day. Have a think about your art, food tech, science, and English assignments. Is there a way to get top marks for your project while also getting the message out about animal rights?

Artwork by Jessica Henderson

INSPIRATION

Zoe Rosenberg (15), San Luis Obispo, California
"I've found there are a lot of vegans who agree with the philosophy of animal rights, but they aren't actively speaking up for animal rights. We need people to speak up. That's how we bring about change."

CRUELTY IN THE CLASSROOM

In my novel, *Amanda the Teen Activist*, Amanda discovers a severe case of animal abuse just outside school grounds. But in real life, many young activists won't even have to look that far. Yup, animal exploitation often happens in schools and colleges.

Sometimes young activists will witness animal cruelty or be forced to participate in animal use at school. Luckily, whether you are a lone activist or standing alongside your team (see Chapter 3), you are now a voice for animals, and you can make a real difference.

Let's take a look at ways animals may be exploited at your school and what steps you can take to help them.

HATCHING PROJECTS

School or kindergarten chick hatching projects involve keeping fertilized eggs in an incubator in the classroom so that kids can watch them hatch and see the little chicks. Ducklings are also used for hatching projects, and the same ethical problems apply.

So What's the Problem?

Cruelty to parent chickens

The fertilized eggs are obtained from a commercial hatchery. The mother and father chickens are kept in factory farm conditions and will never see their chicks. The mother and father chickens will eventually be slaughtered. A mother hen would usually love her fertilized eggs and would even talk to the unhatched chicks as they develop. She would sit on them to keep them warm and gently turn them. But in hatching projects, the chicks are kept in an incubator.

Unsuitable environment for chicks

A classroom is not the right place for a chick to hatch and grow. Sick chicks may not get the veterinary attention they need. They may not be supervised on weekends, and even your most well-intentioned classmates can be too rough and harm the chicks.

Teaching a dangerous lesson

Your classmates can learn a dangerous lesson from watching chicks hatch in a machine. These projects teach that animals are disposable and can be bred without any concern for their lives. Do you think this is a smart lesson? Surely it would be better for your teacher to nurture compassion in the classroom by encouraging respect for life and teaching that animals are a lifelong commitment and responsibility.

Unhappy endings for the chicks

Once the project is over, the teacher has to decide what to do with the chicks. One option is to give them back to the hatching project company. If they do this, the chicks either go into factory farms or are killed immediately. A lot of schools don't feel comfortable with this, so they try to rehome the chicks to parents. Who wouldn't want to adopt a beautiful, fluffy chick? The problem is most parents are under pressure to take the chicks without having a chance to think it through. They may love the idea of chickens now, but they probably haven't budgeted for vet bills down the line, and they almost never have a plan for roosters who crow and who aren't allowed to be kept in suburban areas.

Dumped chickens and broken hearts

Kids often bond with the chickens and are heartbroken when they are taken away.

Hatching projects put huge pressure on sanctuaries. An amazing activist called Bede runs a sanctuary in New South Wales, Australia, called A Poultry Place. He gets contacted daily about unwanted chickens from hatching projects. Roosters make a lovely, loud crowing sound, which people just love to moan about, so often people keep the hens and dump the roosters. This is devastating for both the roosters and the hens, who are bonded after growing up together. Sometimes people dump roosters in the wild where they can be eaten by predators, starve to death, or get caught by the rangers and put down. Other times people take the roosters to the vet to be killed.

And all because of an ineffective school project. I have met some incredible chickens who were saved from hatching projects. Little Gregory, pictured on the next page, was skilled at finding the comfiest spots to relax on and loved a chin scratch.

HATCHING PROJECT ALTERNATIVES

» Search YouTube for "chick hatching," and you will find hundreds of videos suitable for showing the class.
» Visit a farm sanctuary.
» Order a model egg kit to see how eggs develop without using living eggs.
» Go bird watching to learn more about birds in the wild.
» Watch live videos of rescued farmed animals at Explore.org/livecams/farm-sanctuary.

It could be that your school is already planning a hatching project or, even worse, is already running one. Not to fear—activists are here!

Next, you will discover how to create a campaign to stop a hatching project going ahead and what to do if a hatching project is already underway. Although this shows how to run a campaign against a hatching project, the following info can act as a campaign template for any issue you want to tackle.

HATCHING A PLAN: CREATING CHANGE WITH CLEVER CAMPAIGNS

Step 1 — Research Your Topic

Before creating a campaign, be sure to get your facts straight. Spend some time researching the topic. Research organizations that have worked on similar campaigns before and see what inspiration you can take from them. At this point you can also come up with a name for your campaign. For example, we could call this "Hatching a Bad Idea."

Step 2 — Set a Goal

After your research, you may have a better idea of what you want to gain from your campaign. Even though we really want the whole world to go vegan and for all hatching projects to stop this minute, we will probably have more success if we set a strategic goal. When setting goals, keep the acronym SMART in mind. Your goals should be Specific, Measurable, Attainable, Realistic, and Time bound. In this case, we could set three goals. Notice how each goal follows the SMART guidelines.

» Find safe homes for current hatching project chicks by deadline.
» Stop school hatching project from going ahead next year by end of current hatching project.
» Get school to sign pledge to agree not to take part in future hatching projects.

Step 3 — Ask

Always start by asking for what you want. Who knows? You might be successful. After doing your research and choosing your goal, take this book or other research you have gathered to school and talk to your teacher about why you think hatching projects are not a good idea. Show them the key points. Remain calm and polite, and stick to the facts. If your teacher presents arguments, listen before calmly responding.

Since you have researched the issue, you will be well-equipped to have a conversation about it. You can do this on your own, or you can go with your animal rights team, a friend, or a parent. You may need to set up an appointment with your teacher or principal. If this is successful, well done, you! If not, don't give up. Give yourself a pat on the back for trying, and move onto the next step.

Step 4 — Petition

A petition is a written request to do/change something, accompanied by as many names and signatures as possible from people who support your cause. It should be addressed to the decision maker, such as your teacher or principal. When you present it to them, it says, "Hey, look how many of us care about this issue. Please pay attention."

In this case, you could have the request written at the top of the page, e.g., *Woollybutt High—Please say no to hatching projects*. Under that you can write a brief summary of what you are asking for and why. You can then have a space where people can write their names and signatures. Approach as many of your classmates and teachers as possible. Explain the problems with hatching projects and ask them to sign your petition. I bet a load of your friends and classmates care about animals, and they may not realize there is anything wrong with hatching projects until you tell them.

When you present the petition to your teacher and they see how many people feel as you do, they may reconsider their actions.

Photo courtesy of Charlize Reynierse

Roosters, rescued from a hatching project, safe at A Poultry Place sanctuary.
Photo courtesy of A Poultry Place.

Are they still ignoring you? Geez!

Step 5A — Call in the Press

Most towns have a newspaper that covers local issues. Look for the contact number, which is usually on the first inside page of the paper or the "about" page of a website. Call them up and explain what is happening at the school and why it is a problem. Tell the journalist about the petition and ask if they would come out and do a story. This media attention may be enough to persuade your school to change its mind. For more info on creating a press release, see page 173.

Step 5B — Social Media

To gain more support for your campaign, you can create a social media page dedicated to it. Create posts explaining the issues and show what people can do to help. Encourage your friends to like and share your posts. The more support you can get, the easier it will be to bring about change.

Step 5C — Protest

If you have enough people on the animals' side, a peaceful protest at your school could be the way forward. You could combine this with other parts of Step 5 (inform the local paper about the protest and create an event page on social media).

Success?

If you have not yet been successful, don't despair. Get together with your activist team and see what other campaign ideas you can think of. Let us know using #SavingAnimals.

Photo courtesy of A Poultry Place

Too Late?

If you learned about the hatching project after the eggs arrived, then you can still take action.

Talk to your teacher about why you feel these little lives matter and why they should not run a hatching project again. It is essential to use this opportunity to try and stop future hatching projects. You can use the NSW Hen Rescue resource here: Henrescue.org/hatching-projects.

Now we need to ensure the animals are safe. Talk to your teacher about who will care for the chicks when the school is closed over the weekend. And ask what they plan to do at the end of the project. Be sure the teacher understands that the chicks will be exploited and killed if they are given back to the hatching project company.

If parents are willing to adopt the chicks, they need to know how to care for hens and roosters. They should be aware that there is a fifty-fifty chance of the chicks being roosters, and that the commitment is for the life of the chicken. There will also be vet bills down the track. Go to Henrescue.org/hen-care for information on caring for chickens.

As a last resort, you or your teacher may need to find the chicks a safe home at a sanctuary. The problem is sanctuaries get contacted every day about unwanted chicks and roosters, and many are full. If you do find a sanctuary that will offer a loving home to the baby animals, consider doing a fundraiser, such as a vegan bake sale, to help with the cost of caring for the chickens.

"THE GREATNESS OF A NATION CAN BE JUDGED BY THE WAY ITS ANIMALS ARE TREATED." —MAHATMA GANDHI

Ducklings are also exploited for hatching projects.

IF YOU MANAGE TO SAVE THE CHICKS OR STOP A HATCHING PROJECT FROM GOING AHEAD, LET US KNOW: #SAVINGANIMALS

Now let's look at some other school animal issues to which you can apply similar campaign tactics.

CUTTING OUT DISSECTION

Dissection is the act of cutting apart a dead animal or part of a dead animal. At my high school, each student in my biology class was presented with a sheep's eyeball to slice open. The eyeballs were straight from the slaughterhouse. It was upsetting to see their lives disrespected and to know everything those poor sheep had been through. I was allowed to sit that class out and leave the classroom. You do not have to participate in dissection, and it is not necessary for your studies.

The first step is to talk to your teacher and explain your feelings about dissection. You can say that:

Dissection teaches disrespect for life.

Dissection causes suffering of animals.

There are better methods of teaching biology, such as computer simulations, videos, and models. You could even watch a vet perform needed operations on their patients rather than cut apart deteriorating animals that were killed for dissection.

INSPIRATION

When **Zoe Rosenberg (15) of San Luis Obispo, California**, refused to dissect a live worm in her class, the teacher went on to get rid of dissection altogether. Go, Zoe!

AG PROGRAMS: TOO CRUEL FOR SCHOOL

Some schools have agriculture programs in which kids learn to keep farmed animals. This may seem pretty cool at first. I mean, you get to hang out with gorgeous animals and learn to care for them. But you see, that's the thing: They are not really being cared for; they are being used.

I bet you know kids in your school who love these animals. Maybe you love these animals. If you have spent time with them, it is only natural that you will have established a bond, much like you would with a dog or a cat. Not only that, but these animals will have bonded with the students. There will come a day when the animals will go to slaughter and be killed, and that day will be the most terrifying, hideous day you could imagine. It is a tragic betrayal to rip their lives away.

Keeping ag animals is exploitation, but it's also not a realistic representation of how animals are used for food today. Animals used in our food system are kept in factory farms where they cannot express natural behaviors. If the teacher truly wanted a student to learn the whole process, the class would go to a slaughterhouse, too. Why don't they? Because it would probably traumatize the class.

Hannah McKay (16) of Orange, New South Wales, Australia, says, "My school had an ag program. I had to do it, but I didn't partake in any bits I thought were inappropriate. I was only thirteen, and I bonded tremendously with the animals. There were calves we cared for that grew up to be cows. Chicks we cared for that grew up to be chickens. I fed them, I cared for them, I really loved them. Once they were killed, I was a mess. I bond very strongly with animals, and it was just heartbreaking. I had betrayed them."

Kevin Courtney Black (22) of California says, "Early in high school I joined Future Farmers of America (FFA) because I thought they were an organization that provides a safe haven for animals. I thought the work I was doing with them was to help animals live happily. Then, as I started rising through the ranks of FFA, I realized I had completely the wrong idea. It wasn't about saving animals, it was about exploiting them. I quit soon after. If your school runs an agricultural program and you are worried about what is going to happen to the animals, I would suggest rallying students together and marching up to the vice principal and principal's office and strongly voicing your concerns for the animals."

For **Charlize Reynierse (22) of Sydney, Australia**, her experience working on her school farm was a big part of what led her to become vegan and an animal rights activist.

> I've always loved spending time with animals, and so when I was at school I jumped at the chance to work on my high school's farm. I used to help take care of the chickens and sheep.
>
> I had a favorite sheep called Mary. I would take her out every day and sit with her under a tree. We'd chill out together for my lunch break. I was severely bullied throughout primary school and high school, and Mary felt like my only friend. She was a kind and loving sheep. Her calm personality helped me to feel calmer. She felt like a friend.
>
> Every year, the sheep would have lambs. Male lambs were

sent to slaughter, and female lambs would be kept to be bred. Mary was a good mum who was relaxed about motherhood. She was known to always have male lambs, which means her babies would always be taken from her. I found this upsetting, as I always bonded with Mary's lambs.

It was Mary's last year at the school. They told me she was going into retirement, but I think it is more likely that she went to slaughter. I really wanted her last lamb to be a girl so she would be able to live. Mary ended up having another boy. I named him Milo, and I got very attached to him. One day both Milo and Mary were taken and I definitely did not eat lamb during that period.

Steggles is a big chicken-meat company here in Australia, and I had to participate in a Steggles program. They give the school Cornish Cross chicks to raise and fatten up for the Sydney Royal Easter Show. It was a competition, and we would be judged on the chickens' live weight and their carcass weight. I took part in the competition twice. I had to weigh the chickens twice a day, weigh what they were eating, and make graphs. Whilst I was doing it I distinctly remember saying, "I would love to be one of these chickens; all they do is eat and sleep. That's the life." It was so different from how I think now. I remember being encouraged to view the chickens as food as opposed to individuals throughout the process of raising them. I didn't spend much time with them because it was such a stressful time in my school life. I think if I was in a better mindset and not being bullied by the people at the farm I probably would have spent more time with the chickens and gotten to know them.

When the Easter Show came around, I hated being there. I felt so anxious. The day the chickens were going to be slaughtered I remember feeling extremely uncomfortable. I placed second. My teacher came up to me and said, "Do you want to see the carcasses?" and I said, "No, thanks." I was very upset. I didn't quite know why I was upset, but I felt sick. It felt all wrong how excited my teacher was and that this moment was being celebrated. I didn't tell anyone how I felt about it as everyone always made fun of me about being sensitive about the animals. Overall it was a horrible time.

We also had to look after dairy cows from Leppington Pastoral Company. The program was called Cows Create Careers. We had to make videos about the process and enter competitions. We had to raise the dairy calves, and then they got sent back to the farm. It was another example of bonding with animals and then having them torn away from me. That is where the connection started.

In the middle of year eleven, I moved schools and moved away from the farm. The area we moved to was rural, so we bought some chicks from a hatchery. This is something I would not do now, as I know the ethical issues with that and that the male chicks are killed. I have always loved chickens, and I could not wait to get my own. I started thinking that if I loved these chickens so much, why am I eating other chickens? I had these thoughts, but I would always drown them out in my head. I would justify my actions by thinking things like, "Well, we have to eat something." I wasn't arguing with anyone other than myself.

I started my own YouTube book channel, and as I spent more time on YouTube I was exposed to more videos. That year, when I was seventeen, I stumbled upon a "Reasons Why I'm Vegan" video. I went on a YouTube binge and watched all the recommended videos. I eventually stumbled upon a short documentary. It was four minutes of footage that showed what happens to animals in agriculture. After watching that, I went vegetarian overnight. I was mostly vegan; I was just eating cheese and chocolate. At this point I was researching more and more. I kept saying to myself I would go vegan after the HSC [high school certificate]. My mum wasn't cooking for me anymore, so it was quite a challenge to deal with whilst also studying for the HSC. I said I'll make the last step after the HSC. Then I watched a video where a calf is taken from his mother dairy cow. The calf is put into a vehicle and looks out the window as he is taken from his mother. The mother is chasing after the calf, and it is heartbreaking. You can see the bond being torn apart. I realized this is what the calves and mothers I had helped care for had been through. That made me say, "No, I am being selfish, I am going vegan now."

SAVING AG ANIMALS

When you learn that your school's agriculture animals are going to be killed, you are probably going to feel confused, angry, powerless, and overwhelmed. These are all normal feelings, but you are not powerless. You can make a difference.

You can apply the steps we looked at for our hatching project campaign to save the ag animals. You just need to make a few tweaks.

Bear in mind the teachers at a school with an ag program may have the attitude that animals are just there to be used. They may not realize that the animals have distinct personalities and that they want to live. This means you will have to work a little harder. So, first things first: Set a goal, and then talk to your teachers. Voice your concern. Raise the animals' voices.

Get Creative

To make this more effective, you could get creative and make a book about the animal(s) in question. Take photos, draw pictures, even make a video. This could show the animal's personality and why they mean so much to you. This is a great project to do with your activist team. You can then share the book with teachers, parents, and other students when you are trying to gain support and are collecting signatures for your petition.

You may find that contacting a large animal rights organization can help your campaign. You can also contact sanctuaries to see if they can offer a home for the animals so you have an option lined up when you talk to the teachers.

If previous steps have been unsuccessful, you may have some luck with an online petition. Go to Change.org/start-a-petition to create a petition to save the animals. You could arrange for an email to be sent to the principal every time someone signs the petition. Try to get as many people from your school and community to sign as possible. Contact animal rights groups in your country or state and ask them to share your link. Suggest that more could be learned from the animals if they stay alive. For example, the school could teach respect and compassion for animals and that animals are not disposable.

If All Else Fails …

When **Zoe Rosenberg (15), of San Luis Obispo, California**, found out that animals were being butchered for a meat-processing class at California Polytechnic State University, she knew she had to act. On April 13, 2018, Zoe entered the slaughterhouse and sat with a pig as a form of civil disobedience.

Zoe livestreamed the protest to bring more attention to the plight of the pig and later posted about her experience on her social media page.

"TODAY I SAT DOWN IN A SLAUGHTERHOUSE WITH A BABY PIG. I DEMANDED THAT THEY RELEASE HER TO OUR SANCTUARY. I REFUSED TO LEAVE. HUNDREDS OF PEOPLE WERE CALLING THE SLAUGHTERHOUSE. THE POLICE CAME AND DRAGGED ME OUT, PROTECTING THE ANIMAL ABUSERS. WE NAMED THE PIG DANA. FOR ABOUT THIRTY MINUTES, WE GAVE HER LOVE, COMPASSION, AND RESPECT. BUT ULTIMATELY, THEY WILL [KILL HER]. WE WILL NEVER FORGET HER. WE WILL HONOR HER LIFE, AND FIGHT FOR ANIMAL LIBERATION. WE WILL FIGHT FOR HER."

Even though Dana's story is very sad, when Zoe realized she could not free Dana, she still did whatever she could to bring attention to what Dana was experiencing. Dana's story was viewed and shared thousands of times.

SCHOOL ANIMALS

It is common for schools to keep animals in the classroom. In my primary school, they kept gerbils and stick insects. The trouble is the school may not provide the best environment for the animals. They may not have a budget for vet bills, and the animals may not be safe over the weekends or school holidays. In fact, I remember many times that the animals did not make it back alive from holiday care with students.

Check over your class companion animals to see if they seem stressed out.

Answer these questions:

> » Do the animals have a place to hide and get away from the staring eyes of the class?
> » Do they have a companion of their own species?
> » Do they have an interesting environment that is as spacious as possible?
> » Could toys be added?
> » Do they have a healthy diet suited to their species?
> » How are they cared for on weekends or over the holidays?
> » Who does the animal's health checks?
> » What will happen if the animal becomes ill?

Do some research on the species of the animal so you have a good idea about their care needs. You can then present your findings to the teacher. A good idea is for the whole class to be provided with a leaflet on the care of the animal. It could even be a class project to create an interesting environment for the animal and to come up with ideas to make his/her life even better.

If you feel the animal is suffering in the school environment, you may want to talk to your teacher about rehoming him/her to a safe, loving home or sanctuary.

It is important not to breed or buy while stray animals die. There are so many small animals seeking homes in rescue centers that it would be very sad for a school to breed from the animals and bring more lives into the world that they do not have a home for. You can provide your school with information to help them make kinder choices.

Edward the rescued mouse

SCHOOL TRIPS TO ZOOS, AQUARIUMS, OR FARMS

School trips can be pretty fun, but not if there is animal exploitation involved. Zoos and aquariums are like prisons for animals.

Conditions for the animals are often dismal, and even in lush-looking enclosures you will see signs of a mental illness called *zoochosis*. Zoochosis is a sign of stress, which shows in symptoms such as animals pacing back and forth or repeating certain behaviors.

Conservation programs are usually just an excuse for the zoo to breed cute baby animals and then keep them captive. Perhaps they are trying to preserve a species, but they have little concern for the individuals within that species.

In my school, we went to both a beef farm and a dairy farm. But it wasn't a real learning experience. We met the cows, but all the horror was kept hidden. They aren't going to show you dehorning or separation of mother and calf. They want to make it seem like nothing bad happens.

If there is a school trip to a zoo or farm, you can choose whether you wish to participate or not. If you decide to go, you could use it as a fact-finding mission. Make notes, take photos, even make a vlog about your experience. Present your findings to your teacher and suggest that, next time, your class could take a trip to an animal sanctuary and meet animals who have been rescued from abusive situations.

FOOD FIGHT!

We speak about food advocacy in Chapter 6, but what about your school tuck shop or cafeteria? Despite the health benefits of fruit, veg, and vegan food, not all schools cater to vegans. Campaigning for more vegan options is a great way to make it easier for your classmates to go vegan.

If your school is having a fundraising sausage sizzle, ask if they can provide veggie hotdogs, too. Vegan hotdogs are yummy with onions, ketchup, and mustard.

ANIMAL ACTION

Google some of your friends' favorite school meals and find vegan versions. Print copies and present them to your school canteen.

As you can see throughout this chapter, every time you want to change something at your school you can use the same campaign structure:

Research the issue.
Choose a goal.
Ask for what you want.
Distribute leaflets and petitions.
Use social media to gain support.
Call local media.
Protest.
Contact a larger animal charity for help.

Have a think about how you could tweak this list to campaign on issues in your school or community.

Blue spreading her wings after being liberated from a battery cage

CHAPTER 5

BE A SUPERSTAR FOR ANIMALS

Your Facebook, Instagram, Twitter, Tumblr, or TikTok profiles give you an excellent opportunity to get the animal rights message out to all your friends and family. Who knows? Your posts may even go viral and reach hundreds of thousands of people.

WHAT'S RIGHT FOR YOU?

If you like to write, why not **start a blog**? You can write about how you feel about animals and what is happening to them. You could start a vegan recipe blog or an activism blog, or you could combine your other hobbies and write about being a vegan football player or a vegan book lover.

If you are happy to be on camera, you could **make videos** and upload them onto YouTube. They could be funny videos, if you are a bit of a comedian, or they can be more serious. Just be yourself; let your personality shine through and get your message out there.

Perhaps you want to make videos about a campaign you are working on, such as saving the ag animals at your school. Or maybe you want to talk about being vegan. You might want to create funny skits, cook a vegan recipe, show what you've been eating, or have a debate with a friend.

If you prefer not to be on camera, you could **record your own podcast**. Have a chat with a vegan friend about hot animal rights topics, interview your vegan heroes, or make it a solo project and talk to your audience about your vegan life.

If you fancy yourself a bit of a photographer, you could **use Instagram** to post pics of rescued animals you've met at farm sanctuaries, or pics of your vegan food.

You may already have a presence on social media sites, and by posting about what is important to you, as well as your other interests, you may help your friends learn what really happens to animals.

TikTok Activism

Kenia (15) and Bianca Jade (12) Bizzocchi of Italy are always on the search for the most effective way to speak up for animals. While they love to speak to people face-to-face about animal rights, they have found that social media enables them to reach many more people. They set up accounts on Instagram, Facebook, and TikTok using the name *Vegan Sisters*, and they post in both English and Italian.

The most recent addition to the girls' activism toolkit was TikTok. Here's what they say about their TikTok strategies.

When starting with TikTok, our goal was to reach as many people as possible, especially young people like us. We look for trending songs and learn the dance, and then we put a twist to it by attaching a vegan question or message. For example, we ask, "Where is the difference between a dog and a pig?" or "Why do you eat meat, dairy, and eggs?" We attach messages like "Love and kindness for all kinds" or "All animals are our besties." The purpose of choosing trending songs is to reach people that we normally wouldn't and also get on the "For You" page of TikTok, which is the page where people who do not follow you see your videos.

We also make videos where we answer comments and questions, and we are planning on doing one-minute vegan cooking videos as well.

We believe that it is important to use social media to speak up for animals because in the generation we are growing up in, everyone uses social media, and it is simply the best and fastest way to spread a message to all types of people all over the world. Although we prefer to participate in direct outreach where we have the opportunity to speak with people face-to-face, using social media allows us to continue doing activism even when we are unable to get out and about. This proved to be fundamental during the COVID-19 lockdown. Seeing how the situation is progressing in Italy and throughout the world, the use of social media will become more and more essential to informing people why we need to end the exploitation of all animals.

Since TikTok videos are often short and fun, you may think they won't have much of an impact for animals, but Kenia and Bianca Jade were surprised to find they were really making a difference. "Many kids our age ask us about going vegan. They either do not know how to start or are having difficulty getting permission from their parents. We reassure these kids and give them advice about healthy vegan food. We also suggest that they get as informed as they can about why being vegan is important for their health, the environment, and the animals. When they are ready, we tell them to make a presentation for their parents, watch documentaries like *What the Health, The Game Changers, Cowspiracy,* and *Dominion* together, and help their parents understand that going vegan is not only safe but a much better choice for everyone. Seeing that we can make a difference in the life of one person or animal at a time makes us feel happy."

Vegan Sisters' TikTok Tips

There are many ways to use TikTok to speak up for the animals. Here are a few suggestions from Kenia and Bianca Jade.

- » Search for trending dances and make your own video with an animal rights message.
- » Make a sixty-second cooking video showing easy and amazing vegan recipes.
- » Ask or answer questions on veganism or animal rights.
- » Do a mini-interview with someone who inspires you.
- » Try a new vegan food and review it.
- » Create a life hack TikTok—for example, showing how aquafaba

could be used instead of eggs.

» Find your passion, be creative, have fun, and use it to spread your message of love and kindness for all kinds.

An unexpected bonus for Kenia and Bianca Jade (pictured above with Cherry Pie) was that some of their social media connections became real-life friends. "We have definitely met many people from all over the world as a result of our use of Facebook, Instagram, and TikTok. This has also led to so many amazing direct experiences with other people who hope to use their voices to end the unnecessary abuse of animals. For example, last year we were contacted by an animal activist from Sicily. She is an English teacher, and she invited us to speak to her students. Through her, we organized a six-week activism tour throughout Sicily, where we participated in Cubes and vigils, cleaned beaches, and met so many wonderful new friends. Social media has also given us the opportunity to contact other young animal activists like ourselves. Last winter, we met Vegan Evan and the Veggie Brothers when visiting our grandparents in Florida. We often make friends with animal sanctuaries and interact with small, ethical companies and help them to promote their cause. Meeting and communicating with all of these kind and interesting people is the best part of being on social media."

Follow Kenia and Bianca Jade on ...

TikTok @vegan.sisters

Facebook @vegansisters

Instagram @_vegansisters_

GRAPHIC IMAGES?

Graphic images or videos of what happens to animals are what prompt many people to make an emotional connection and go vegan. I bet you could find loads of people who never would have become vegan if it weren't for these videos.

I went veg when I found out that meat is made from an animal. But it took more for me to go vegan. I was exposed to some graphic footage of what happens in the egg and dairy industries, and after that I knew there was no way I wanted to contribute to that suffering. Sometimes after I have watched graphic footage, I feel a renewed motivation to take action for the animals. When I am confronted by the truth, it gives me the kick up the bum I need to get things done. It reminds me of the urgency of the situation. I also feel that way every time I enter a place where animals are exploited.

The other thing that can happen when people see graphic images or footage is that they can become disgusted or overwhelmed, and they may turn away. They may block you from their socials so they don't see any more images. This isn't ideal because if they block you, how will you reach them in the future?

The thing is, different things work for different people. But when people get offended by these images and videos, it is important to remember that they are offended by the very thing they are paying others to do.

So it's up to you what angle you take. Many animal rights activists already have a strong online presence, but there is always room for new voices.

DIFFERENT PEOPLE SPEAK TO DIFFERENT PEOPLE

Whether you are shy and prefer to hide behind a blog, or are super outgoing and want to make a vlog every day, there is a place for you online. Don't feel you have to be a certain size, gender, shape, age, or race to be an online activist.

INSPIRATION

Bailey Mason (16), Sydney, Australia

@WarriorforAnimals

I use social media to reach people and tell them the truth about what is happening to animals. It makes it really easy for people to get involved with my campaigns from anywhere in the world. Sometimes, I even have to translate my comments. The big business of animal agriculture does not like activists being on social media because it is so easy for us to expose what they're doing. It creates this big community of people saying, "No, it's not okay to use and abuse animals."

I campaign against all kinds of animal abuse, but my focus is on ending dolphins in captivity—in particular, one facility in Coffs Harbour called Dolphin Marine Magic. Social media enables me to tell everyone what's going on at that facility and the cruelty to the dolphins.

Dolphin Marine Magic have their Twitter account on private now. I guess they're not happy with people knowing that they keep dolphins and other animals in small pools. Social media is an amazing tool for young activists and can truly make a difference and better the world.

Bailey's Social Media Tips

> Think about what you're going to post ahead of time. Jot down all the ideas that come into your head onto a piece of paper. From there, you can choose your best ideas and use that as the starting point for your social media strategy.

If you get negative reactions to your posts, that's okay. It doesn't matter what people say. A lot of the time, the people commenting don't even know you. What matters is that you're doing the right thing.

Try to focus on all the positive feedback you get and take the opportunity to make connections with other activists. The negativity comes from the animal abuse industries' misinformation and lies. The positive comments are coming from the truth. The truth is that animal abuse is wrong.

ANIMAL ACTION

If you already have a social media account, create a post telling people the truth about what happens to animals. If you don't have a social media account, choose your preferred platform and set up your account.

INSPIRATION

Ateret Goldman (16), Berkeley, California

I was scrolling through my Facebook feed, and I saw a post with a photo of two people behind a table, holding signs against animal abuse. The post said, "Doing vegan outreach on Pearl Street Mall." This was in my local area at the time.

I was inspired, and I commented, "I want in." We started messaging, and that's how I got into vegan outreach and activism.

Since it was a social media post that brought me to activism, I know how important it is, and that is what I am called to do now. Facebook, Instagram, and YouTube are amazing tools to share animals' stories and to inspire and mobilize people. It is so easy to get our message out.

Saying that, a lot of your success will depend on how many people you reach. That's why I work a lot on getting videos to go viral. I think about viral ideas before doing anything on social media. I think, "Is this idea one that people will care about? Is this something that will motivate people to take action, such as coming to an event or signing a petition?"

For example, recently two piglets were saved from a Smithfield farm. Their names are Lily and Lizzy. The FBI have spent hundreds of thousands of dollars trying to find these piglets. They have even raided sanctuaries and scared and hurt the animals there. It's outrageous. These sweet piglets were saved from a horror show by Direct Action Everywhere, and now the rescuers are made to feel like criminals, and the piglets are seen as property.

It was important that we tell the story of these piglets in an interesting way. One of the tools we successfully harnessed was protest. When planning a protest we could have just gone to Costco, which sells pig flesh from Smithfield, and we could have held signs that say, "Lily deserves to live" and done some chants, but it wouldn't get so many shares on social media.

Instead, we thought creatively. What if we went to Costco and showed actual footage of the farm Lily was saved from? What if we then showed Lily free at the sanctuary? What if we then said, "You have a choice. Do you want to support the FBI who are attacking this piglet, or are you going to let her live at the sanctuary?"

We need to tell these animals' stories and show people the truth of what corporations are paying millions to hide. If you are successful in telling the story of an individual animal, the post is more likely to go viral.

Lily was rescued by Direct Action Everywhere.
Photo courtesy of Direct Action Everywhere.

Tips to Make Viral Posts

Think creatively. How can you help people connect with the individual animal, such as sweet little Lily?

Concentrate on the individual. People are more likely to connect with one named animal rather than a large herd or flock. Every animal has his/her own unique personality, and sharing that via social media will go a long way toward helping people connect with their story.

Upskill. Get the skills you need for the social media you are working on. Ateret took a twenty-hour course on how to edit video with Final Cut Pro software. Could you take an editing course? Maybe a photography or design course may help?

Reach out to experienced activists. For example, for video editing you could reach out to Ateret for advice.

TIP

Look at other activists' social media accounts. You don't want to copy them, but maybe they will give you ideas. Here are some great accounts on Instagram to follow:

@WarriorforAnimals @GenesisButler_ @VeganEvan @HaileThomas @nswhenrescue @dzvegankidathletes @jessicajaneillustrations @weareveganuary @aiyana.goodfellow @_vegansisters_

INTERNET TROLLS

There's no doubt that the internet provides great opportunities to build a supportive community and learn loads about animal issues. The problem is that it is also a place where people write mean things that they would probably never say to your face. Some people will purposefully cause trouble by making mean comments on your feed. They are called *trolls*, and the golden rule is *Don't Feed the Trolls* by replying to their comments. The more you engage with them, the more they will comment. The more popular your socials get, the more likely it is you will attract trolls, so it is best to be prepared.

Katie Lynch-Dombroski (17), Denver, Colorado, says, "Don't engage with internet trolls. Try to ignore their negativity and stay true to yourself. Think about why you are vegan in the first place. Know your true intentions and do not get intimidated by people. Be gentle with yourself and don't get caught up in perfection."

Jasmine Shaw (18), Central Coast, Australia, had a hard time from some peers at school when she reviewed a vegan restaurant online. Here is what she learned from her experience: "I got a lot of hate messages and comments. It has improved now. I think as I've got older, I have learned how to be vocal without attracting people who will be difficult. I choose where I will advocate. I still put animal rights stuff on my Facebook feed all the time, but if someone says anything negative or trolls my feed, I block them straightaway. I can tell if someone is asking a genuine question or if they are just trolling."

CHAPTER 6

FOOD FOR THOUGHT

Some people think that all vegans eat is soggy kale and lentils. The truth is that vegans have a huge variety of food to choose from. Pretty much any non-vegan food you can think of can be recreated vegan—from cookies and ice cream to lasagna, tacos, and burgers. Anything non-vegans can eat, we can eat vegan.

So one way to help people open up to veganism is to show them how much yummy food vegans can eat. Sharing vegan food is simple, delicious, and effective and can spark some great conversations.

But how does sharing vegan food help the animals?

As you've seen in earlier chapters, being vegan is just about the best way to limit the harm you do to animals. The more people become vegan, the more animals are spared. The thing is, not everyone is open to becoming vegan because they think there will be nothing good to eat.

When you show people that vegans can eat a wide range of yummy food *and* meet their nutritional needs, it breaks down that barrier and allows you to have a conversation with them.

Perhaps someone who has eaten some of your vegan food will go on to meet another vegan who talks to them about the animals, and they will be more open to the conversation.

Perhaps you have already tried talking to your friends and family about animals, and they just aren't interested. So now is the time to let the vegan cupcakes do the talking. Plus, when they have their mouth full, they can't argue as easily.

Food activism can range from a fundraising vegan sausage sizzle to sharing healthy and delicious vegan food with people in need. It may seem like it's all about food, but it really is #SavingAnimals and helping people.

Kevin Courtney Black (22) of California says, "Veganism is growing by the minute, and as more people go vegan we get new vegan recipes and food. I love cooking and baking, so getting the opportunity to try a new recipe is always great. Sharing that food with others is a way to spread the love that is veganism and our message for peace."

FREE-FOOD ACTIVISM

Vegan Evan of Florida is a seven-year-old activist. He does all kinds of different things to help animals. In fact, he is co-president and spokesperson for Animal Hero Kids, an organization that reaches more than 30,000 kids and teens a year with a message of kindness.

One kind of activism Evan does with Animal Hero Kids is free-food activism. He gives out samples of vegan food along with leaflets on how to be vegan. What a great way to reach out to people. After all, everyone loves free food.

Vegan Evan says, "It's good because people like the food. It surprises them because it tastes so good, and then they are more open to reading the leaflet about what happens to animals to make meat, eggs, and dairy. In the booklet there are cool facts about animals so people can see how great they are. It includes studies that show animals have feelings and emotions."

"When people meet me, they get to know me and they see I am a happy, healthy kid and I'm vegan. It helps them see that if I can do it, then so can they. Some people think going vegan is really hard, but it wasn't difficult for me. I just looked at meat, eggs, and dairy and thought, 'If eating this hurts animals, then I don't want to do it.' I still have pizza and cupcakes now, but they're vegan. At first, my grandpa wasn't sure about veganism. We made him delicious vegan food and asked him to watch movies like *Cowspiracy* and other animal and health movies. Now he's vegan!"

I love Vegan Evan's idea of giving out delicious vegan food along with information. Okay, it's kind of like a bribe, but people won't be complaining once they taste your food.

If you want to take it a step further, you could even offer a vegan cupcake if someone is willing to sit down and watch a few minutes of footage of what happens to animals.

FEEDING THE HOMELESS: HUMANS ARE ANIMALS, TOO

Feeding the homeless is really important. That is why it's so awesome that organizations like Food not Bombs, Chilis on Wheels, and A Well-Fed World exist. These charities feed the hungry without exploiting animals. They make big batches of healthy, filling vegan food and distribute it to those in need. They also prepare food for homeless people's dogs.

DID YOU KNOW?

Usually homeless people aren't allowed to take their dogs into homeless shelters. Many of these people choose to stay on the streets rather than give up their companions. Maybe you could help homeless people in your community. Contact one of the organizations below for advice on how to get started.

Chilisonwheels.org
Foodnotbombs.net
Awfw.org

Priscilla Huynh (20) of Sydney, Australia, found sharing delicious food to be effective in helping her family to understand her veganism.

My family did not react well when I said I wanted to go vegan. They were unsupportive and would continually offer me animal products. I tried to share what I had learnt about the agriculture industry with them, but they kept telling me veganism was a bad idea and that all my research was propaganda. It was mentally draining trying to convince them when they didn't really want to learn. Instead of arguing, I now make my family vegan food to show them how delicious it can be.

One of my hobbies has always been baking, and when I went vegan I was determined to bake delicious vegan treats. I was unsure where to begin as I had never eaten a vegan cake before. I found an easy vegan vanilla cupcake recipe online, followed the instructions, and it turned out to be delicious. You would never be able to tell it was vegan. After learning how easy it was to substitute eggs, butter, and dairy milk in recipes using ingredients like oil, aquafaba, applesauce, vegan butter, and soy milk, the possibilities were endless with baking.

I have my own baking side business called Cakenection (follow on Instagram @Cakenection), where I help connect people through eating delicious plant-based food. I also help people make the connection that animals and their secretions are not food. My specialty is custom cakes and 3D-sculpted cakes. I have made a spray paint can that actually sprays edible paint, a koala cake, a 3D-camera cake, and plenty more. It is easy to research and find out what cake decorating products such as food coloring and fondant are vegan friendly. If you are unable to find the information, email the company to check directly.

I find sharing food a fun and effective way to start chatting to people about veganism. I even spent one weekend baking vegan cookies to give to healthcare workers who were stressed out due to COVID-19. I then took them around the hospitals as a treat for the workers.

ACTIVIST PROFILE

Haile Thomas (19), New York City

"HAILE IS AN EXAMPLE FOR ALL OF YOU, WHAT YOUR LITTLE POWERFUL VOICES CAN DO TO CHANGE THE WORLD."
—*MICHELLE OBAMA*

Haile Thomas is an international speaker, blogger, YouTuber, and activist. Is there anything this girl can't do? Not only does she inspire thousands of people to live a healthy, plant-based lifestyle, but she even started her own nonprofit organization, HAPPY (Healthy Active Positive Purposeful Youth). HAPPY teaches kids and teens in schools and underprivileged communities how to eat a healthy plant-based diet. Through her work, Haile is helping people become their healthiest selves while saving the planet and animals, too.

So, Haile, why did you decide to go vegan?

I was doing some research online and stumbled upon an article revealing that red meat turns on cancer genes. That led me to research more. It wasn't long until I fully embraced veganism and all of its benefits for the body, the planet, and the animals. I hated the idea of ever contributing to the decline of my health and well-being, but also to the suffering of other animals and the planet.

What is your favorite vegan food?

Currently, it's got to be mushrooms. I just love how versatile they are, quick to cook and easily adaptable to different flavors and methods of preparation. I particularly love using them in Buddha bowls, salads, curry stews, and even baked crispy to mimic "bacon" but with no harm to pigs.

Why do you think plant-based nutrition education is an important form of activism?

By educating others about the health and healing benefits of a vegan diet, there is great potential to influence behavior changes and empower others to take their health into their hands. This empowerment has a snowball effect of positive change for the planet and for animals. Often, when someone's eyes are opened to a more compassionate, sustainable, delicious, and nutritious way of eating, they are forever changed.

You have created a vegan cookbook. What did you learn from the experience?

Creating my vegan empowerment cookbook, *Living Lively*, was such a joy-filled experience. I absolutely loved testing out recipes and being able to have creative freedom in creating a book that highlighted the importance of all parts of wellness and some delicious recipes. Working with an amazing publisher and getting to do interviews and photoshoots with my friends was a surreal experience. Knowing that *Living Lively* was produced by all kids under twenty-one is something I'm really proud of.

Can you tell me a bit about The HAPPY Organization?

I founded my nonprofit, HAPPY (TheHappyOrg.org), in 2012 after I noticed a severe lack of free or low-cost nutrition and culinary education for kids in my community and all across the country. I believe that quality food education is a birthright and also the key to creating strong, healthy, and empowered leaders. When we eat foods that nourish our bodies, we are fueling our potential. I wanted to empower healthier generations by providing programs and classes for young people that could transfer life-changing information in a fun and engaging way. We give kids this information via classes, workshops, and fun summer camps.

What is one of your most memorable moments with HAPPY?

One of my favorite HAPPY memories is from one of our vegan summer camps a few years ago.

One day we were doing a group cooking activity, and the main vegetable we were using was sweet potato.

As soon as we announced what we were making, one of our most "picky" campers insisted that she was very allergic to sweet potatoes and she couldn't eat them. I was, of course, courteous and told her it was fine if she didn't eat it.

Later in the day, during pick-up, I was chatting with her dad and asked him about her sweet potato allergy. He admitted that she had never even eaten a sweet potato and wasn't allergic at all. I was shocked at first, but then I remembered just how rare it is for many kids to try new and different ingredients on their own, even if it is a basic produce item. The next day, I had a talk with her about the "allergy," and she admitted that she said she was allergic because she was too scared to try it. That same day, I decided that it was important for her to be positively encouraged to try sweet potato. So together we made three dishes, all containing sweet potato. She was tentative at first; eventually she came around to trying it. And she LOVED it. This camper was so happy and couldn't stop eating the potatoes. She found her new favorite food but never would have tried it if she didn't have the access, encouragement, support, and opportunity to try it in a few different ways.

Check out Haile's work at HaileVThomas.com and TheHappyOrg. org.

GET STARTED

Don't worry; if starting your own organization is a bit overwhelming, you can get started with food activism by cooking a healthy and delicious vegan meal for your family, or even make like the Uppertons and grow your own veggies.

Jack Upperton (7) and his sisters, Summer (5) and Grace (4), live in Malaysia. They love to grow their own veggies.

Jack, future vegan chef

Jack says, "Growing your own fruit and veggies makes it even more fun to cook with them or make juices and smoothies. My favorite vegetables to grow and eat are broccoli and carrots, but when Mum is not looking, I like feeding them to the animals, too. When I grow up I want to open a vegan café which will have an animal sanctuary outside so people can meet the animals. We had sheep at the last place I lived, and they were great. Their names were Stella, Emma, and Rainbow."

"If people met the rescued animals, they could get to know their personalities, and I would tell the people, 'Stop eating animals now,' but in an encouraging way. Me and Mum once screened an environmental documentary called *Cowspiracy* that sold out the movie theater. It felt good because people got to know the truth about how meat is cruel and destroys the environment. In my café I will have regular screenings of movies that show what happens with animals, and a community garden so people can see how good veggies are and all the good food you can make."

FEELING INSPIRED?

If you are full of vegan beans after reading about these awesome young food activists, ask yourself what you can do, and start planning to make a difference today.

Here are some ideas:

1. Contact ChilisOnWheels.org **or** FoodNotBombs.net to ask for advice on how to help homeless people in your community.

2. Hand out free vegan food samples with your vegan leaflets.

3. Set up a laptop with footage of what happens in farms and slaughterhouses. **Bake some vegan cupcakes and do a cupcake challenge,** rewarding people with a cupcake if they watch the footage.

4. Choose a recipe from Haile's website: HaileVThomas.com/blog. Tell your family or friends you are making dinner and show them how delicious and healthy vegan food can be. Remember, people will be more open to the animal rights message if they already like the food.

5. Bake cookies or cupcakes and take them to school to give to your classmates. You could even hand out the recipe.

6. If you know a fair bit about healthy vegan nutrition, you could **hold classes in your school** or even **go to local schools** to show people how to cook healthy recipes.

7. If your food looks good, **take pics and post to your Instagram account.** You could even make a recipe video.

CHAPTER 7

GET CREATIVE

Using your skills and talents to help animals

By sharing your creative work, you can challenge people's beliefs about animal rights without causing them to become defensive.

This is why I chose to use my love of creative writing to write a novel, *Amanda the Teen Activist,* which combines an exciting fictional story with an animal rights theme.

Emi Pizarro Zamora reading *Amanda the Teen Activist*

Have a think about your skills, hobbies, and talents. How could they be used for activism?

ANIMAL ACTION

Get a piece of paper and write down all the things you enjoy doing and all your skills.

Maybe you like roller skating and drawing. How could you use these things to help animals? Well, you could create a big animal rights poster with your drawing skills and then go roller skating around town to show it off.

Okay, so maybe not—but check out the inspiration below, and you'll get the idea. Once you see all your hobbies and skills written down, you may be surprised by how easy it is to think of ways you can use these skills to help animals.

WRITING

If you like writing, then you have endless opportunities to write on behalf of the animals. Keep an eye out for local animal issues and write an article about them for your local or school newspaper.

Bailey Mason (16) of Sydney, Australia, says, "I write articles for the online website The Big Smoke. It's part of their Next Generation Program. I was really happy to start that last year. I've written about the dairy industry, pig farming, and everything in between. It's not a vegan website, which means I get to talk about veganism with non-vegans. I think that's really important."

Get Political

Politics and laws should change to reflect the aims of society, but laws are often much slower than the rest of society to move forward. While most people are against cruelty to animals, animal rights often seem to be the very last thing on politicians' minds. Maybe this is because the animals themselves cannot vote. For this reason, it is really important that we use our voices and our creative talents to speak up for animals and let politicians know that animal rights is an important cause.

Lobbying is when you use your voice as a member of the public or as part of an organization to tell the government what you want to happen in your country or state.

One method of lobbying is writing letters. **Charlotte Lim (22) of Sydney, Australia**, has written letters to politicians asking them to ban factory farming.

Charlotte's letter calling for an end to factory farming

```
The Hon. Scott Morrison, MP
Prime Minister
Parliament House
Canberra, ACT 2600


Dear Prime Minister Morrison,


I am appalled at your continued support of Australia's
factory farming industry.

3,854,700,000 shellfish
396,360,000 fish
652,680,000 chickens
28,896,900 sheep
8,241,000 ducks
7,423,300 cows
6,320,000 turkeys
5,159,800 pigs

… are killed each year in Australia in the animal
agriculture industry.

It is unacceptable that these individuals, with lives
that matter to them, are brought into the world
for the purpose of being slaughtered. What is the
difference between dogs and cats, who are protected by
law, and pigs, who have the same level of intelligence
```

as a dog and yet are crammed into metal cages for the sole purpose of being brutally murdered for human consumption?

Humane slaughter is a lie. Animals cannot consent to their deaths.

There are not only more ethical alternatives but more environmentally friendly methods of generating the income wrought from animal agriculture. Diverting investments into plant-based meat and sustainable energy would be far more beneficial to the Australian environment and economy. When we look at the devastating impact of climate change on Australia's very unique ecosystem, it is imperative that Australia makes the transition from a meat-based culture to a vegan one.

Research done by Dr. Kimberly Nicholas and Seth Wynes at Lund University (2017) demonstrates that eating a vegan diet is one of the most effective ways an individual can limit their carbon output. It is the responsibility of national leaders like you to educate the public and implement policies and strategies to ensure that the planet, Australian economy, and human and animal lives remain healthy and prosperous.

Please ban factory farming.

Kind regards,
Charlotte Lim

You can write a letter or an email about pretty much anything you think is important. You could write an email thanking a company for an awesome vegan product, or asking the council to ban animal circuses from exhibiting in the council area. Maybe you could write a letter to the editor of your local paper.

TOP LETTER WRITING TIPS

1. Be polite.

2. Ask for what you want clearly.

3. Use personal stories or examples.

4. Draw on solid facts.

5. Use the correct name and title of the person you are writing to.

6. Use your own words.

7. Don't exaggerate. The abuse of animals is bad enough without making things up.

8. Provide your contact details.

9. Follow up if necessary.

FORM LETTERS

A form letter is a template of a letter that others can use to make their own letter writing easier. When writing a form letter to share with others, you still follow the advice above, but you use fewer personal stories and more facts. You can always advise the people you share it with to add their own personal touch; you're just making things a bit easier for them so people are more likely to take action.

Like Charlotte, **Callan Flynn (11) of Sydney, Australia**, uses letters as a form of activism. He's written many letters asking politicians to ban factory farming and live exports. Check out his letter against live export on the next page.

Callan's form letter calling for an end to live exports

Dear [Politician's Name Here],

Some things are simply indefensible. Allowing an animal to thrash and bellow in pain as he is killed, fully conscious, is definitely one of those things. The fact that your government allows this to happen en masse to animals born into Australian care and then exported as part of our live export trade is shameful.

I understand that economic experts have predicted the live export trade could be phased out with minimal impact to Australian farmers and with significant mid- to long-term benefits to our economy.

But irrespective of any economic pros or cons, the simple fact remains, some things are indefensible. Please ban the cruel live export trade before any more animals must endure such a horrific fate.

Regards,
[Your Name Here]

Callan Flynn and friend

ANIMAL ACTION

Write an email or letter about veganism or an animal issue. It could be a letter to your local paper. It could be a letter to a company asking them to make vegan products. It could be a letter to your local politicians explaining why they should stand up for animals. It doesn't have to be a formal letter; for some companies, a quick email is just as appropriate.

Voting

By going vegan, we are voting with our wallets, but just as important is voting in elections. It is essential to use your right to vote, and in most countries you get the first opportunity to do this at the age of eighteen. It's an exciting chance to be heard.

Have a look at each party and politician and see who aligns most with your views. What are their policies on animal rights? Do they even acknowledge animals? If the candidates do not acknowledge animals, take time to research their other policies on social justice issues. Do they have any anti-wildlife or pro-animal farming policies that may actively harm animals? All this research can help inform whom you decide to vote for. Many elections come very close, and a few votes really can make a difference.

Use Your Voice

In Australia, we have a political party to represent voters who want an end to animal cruelty. It is called the Animal Justice Party (AJP), and it has had three members of Parliament elected in just four years. The AJP gives a political voice to animals around Australia.

You may not have an animal-specific political party in your country, but once you have found a political member that best represents your views, you can help to get them elected by using some of the tactics in this book. Here are a few ways you could get involved in politics for animals:

» Run stalls where you chat to people about animal rights and politics.
» Create and sign petitions to introduce or change bills.
» Leaflet for your chosen political party.
» Hand out how-to-vote cards for your political party on polling day.
» Display a sign on your house for your chosen political member.

There are loads of ways to help. If you live in Australia, you can even join Young AJP, for people aged fourteen to twenty-eight, and take an active role in changing laws for the better.

Submissions and Public Comment

If a government agency is planning to introduce a new law, bill, or regulation, members of the public have a right to make comments and to have those comments heard and noted.

Earlier this year, I had the exciting opportunity to speak up for animals in the NSW House of Parliament. The AJP had tabled an inquiry into animal cruelty laws in NSW, looking at whether authorities such as the police and RSPCA were doing their job of enforcing animal cruelty laws. Submissions were invited from the public. I wrote an eleven-page submission detailing my experiences of reporting animal cruelty to the authorities. I focused on the Lakesland hens case, where, in 2018, a NSW farmer starved and dehydrated 4,000 hens to death and the RSPCA and police did not save a single hen. When NSW Hen Rescue and concerned community members attempted rescue of the hens, the authorities focused on arresting us instead of helping the hens.

The RSPCA inspectors actually cheered as a police officer tackled me to the ground, knocking a dying hen from my arms. I am in favor of establishing a new Independent Animal Welfare Council. This would mean organizations like the RSPCA (which makes money from the meat industry) would not be in charge of investigating animal cruelty.

I was invited to Parliament House in Sydney to attend the inquiry. I sat surrounded by politicians, and they asked me all kinds of questions about my experiences. I was asked questions by members from different parties, even the Shooters, Fishers, and Farmers Party! What a brilliant way to have my voice heard and to speak up for animals. While the bill is still before Parliament, I could be a part of bringing about a massive positive change for animals—and you could, too, if you use your voice.

If you are given a chance to speak up for animals, always use it.

Six of us are appealing the guilty conviction for aggravated trespass that we received when attempting to save the Lakesland hens. If we succeed, this will set a precedent that sometimes it is necessary to trespass in order to attend an emergency situation for animals. If we were attempting to save humans, it would be seen as a necessity and we would not have been charged—why should animals be excluded? It would have been far easier for us to plead guilty and have the case over and done with. Instead, it is still going on more than two years later, but this is a chance to speak up for animals and challenge old and outdated laws. The AJP have been supportive of this decision and believe it could bring about important change.

Challenging Speciesist Laws

It can be really disheartening to see how many politicians do not even acknowledge animals. It seems that the farmers' votes always come first, even with the most sickening practices.

One campaign the AJP is working on is to ban the use of 1080. This awful poison is used to kill foxes in Australia. It causes them to experience the most painful deaths, and many other animals who consume it die, too. Having the AJP in Parliament gives us a much better chance of this issue being heard and laws being changed.

To find out more about the Animal Justice Party, go to AnimalJusticeParty. org.

And, if you're in the U.S., check out the vegan animal rights Humane Party at HumaneParty.org.

CREATIVE WRITING

For me, writing stories is a great way to get active for animals. It's also therapeutic and, I hope, entertaining for readers. **Gemma Krogh (13) of Gosford, New South Wales, Australia**, writes poetry to express her feelings about animals. Gemma performed the poem below at her event, Chicken Acknowledgement Day.

Fallen Hero

by Gemma Krogh

You start off as a hero on top of the wall
You keep talking to yourself telling you that you're tall,
But the people make you feel like you're worth nothing at all,
And a voice in your head keeps telling you you're smaller than you
actually be,
It's deadly, it's poison, it means that you'll never be free,
And as you struggle with yourself you sink under the sea,
And as you fight for your life they're fighting for money.

And the world and the animals will slowly fade away,
If we don't join hands and do something today,
For the only war we'll be fighting if we do join hands,
Will be a war for this world, and for these sacred lands,
You will see a lot more if you open your eyes,
The world isn't just your own stupid lives,
Give a little for the sake,
Of the land from which you take,
And do a lot less to break,
Lives with your mistakes.

ART

"I think art is a great form of activism," says **Emma Black (14) of Wollongong, Australia**. "I started to draw when I saw what was happening to animals. I drew what I thought they were feeling. I started uploading the drawings to social media and sharing them with people. People would ask me questions like, 'What does this represent?' and I would have the perfect opportunity to talk to them about it. I would tell them how scared the animals are in the slaughterhouse. It starts a conversation. Drawing was my first form of activism."

Emma's activist artwork

CHALKING

Emma also uses chalking as a form of activism. "In my area, loads of people get together to go running every weekend," she says. "I got a big box of chalk, and I went down to the beach before sunrise. I did colorful chalk drawings and wrote vegan quotes before the runners started jogging by. It was a great way to get people thinking. They may just glance down at the quote, or they may stop and look carefully at the images and the artwork. Either way, it is planting a seed. I am really interested in art, and I spend a lot of time looking through artwork for ideas for my art or chalking."

It's not just Emma who likes chalking for the animals. Many young activists, including **Khendall Lil Bear (8) of Florida**, find that chalking is a great way to express themselves and advocate for animals. If you're feeling creative, you can make beautiful drawings like Emma's—or you can just write quotes or an animal rights message on the sidewalk. All you need is some chalk. The more colorful, the better.

Khendall's chalk activism

Graffiti is illegal, but chalking will just wash away. As long as you are not annoying a particular business, you can happily chalk away ... just don't do it when it is about to rain.

Head out with some friends to an area where there is a fair amount of foot traffic and where it is safe for you to be. You can write your vegan or animal rights message and even draw some animal pictures to go with it. If there is an animal rights issue in your community, this is another way to draw attention to it.

Your imagination is the only limit when it comes to what you can chalk. Have a look below for inspiration, or check #VeganChalkChallenge on Instagram.

If you want to take your chalking to the next level, you could invest in some stencils from a company like SacredScribble.com. They have stencils you can buy that have ready-made animal rights messages. Simply place the stencil on the surface you have chosen for your message and use a spray chalk to spray over the letters. When you remove the stencil, your animal rights message will be there for all to see.

Use the chalking slogans below for inspiration

Write in big, bold letters. Maybe add a cute drawing of an animal or draw a pattern around the words to attract attention.

You can keep it simple or let your imagination run wild.

Have fun and get chalking!

IN A WORLD WHERE YOU CAN
BE ANYTHING,
BE KIND

IF WE COULD LIVE HAPPY & HEALTHY LIVES WITHOUT
HURTING OTHERS,
WHY WOULDN'T WE?

WATCH "DOMINION"

IN THE EGG INDUSTRY, ALL MALE CHICKS
ARE KILLED AT 1 DAY OLD
BECAUSE THEY DON'T LAY EGGS
EGGSEXPOSED.COM

NEW YEAR'S RESOLUTION - BE VEGAN
VEGANUARY.ORG

THERE IS NO SUCH THING AS "HUMANE MEAT"
ASK ANY ANIMAL

NOT YOUR MUM, NOT YOUR MILK
DITCHDAIRY.COM.AU

ANIMALS ARE HERE WITH US
NOT FOR US

KILLING IS NEVER HUMANE
KILLING IS NEVER GENTLE
KILLING IS NEVER KIND
CHOOSE COMPASSION. CHOOSE VEGAN.

ANIMAL AGRICULTURE IS THE
LEADING CAUSE OF
SPECIES EXTINCTION
WATER POLLUTION &
HABITAT DESTRUCTION
WATCH "COWSPIRACY" ON NETFLIX

IF YOU BELIEVE IT'S WRONG
TO HURT ANIMALS,
YOU ALREADY BELIEVE IN VEGANISM

FISH ARE FRIENDS

PHOTOGRAPHY

Oliver Davenport (17) of Melbourne, Australia, uses photography as activism.

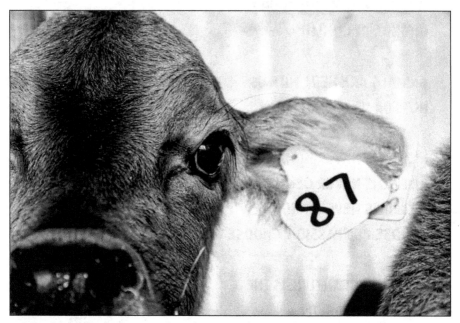

"Could you look an animal in the eye and say to them, 'My appetite is more important than your suffering?'" —Moby

Photo by Oliver Davenport

"At the start of 2017," Oliver says, "I got a camera and started to play around with it. It soon became my main form of activism. I go to dairy farms, saleyards, wherever I can, to take photos. I take photos to show how animals are abused and suffering. I find it is the best way I can get a story out and get people to connect with individual animals."

"Boy on the way to slaughter" by Oliver Davenport

Oliver uses his photography for many forms of activism. "I gathered with twelve others as part of a project called Bear Witness Australia. We go to slaughterhouses, vigils, and protests and take photos of what is happening there. I know these animals are going through such horror—the least I can do is tell their stories. That is why I carefully caption my photos."

"THE TIME WILL COME WHEN MEN SUCH AS I WILL LOOK UPON THE MURDER OF ANIMALS AS THEY NOW LOOK ON THE MURDER OF MEN."
—LEONARDO DA VINCI

"Just a baby. Such innocence. We take that away from her for one meal. Her life for a meal."—Oliver Davenport

MUSIC

For many people, music is a form of self-expression, a way to relax, something to dance to, and a way to connect with our emotions. If you are talented at songwriting or making music, you have a wonderful opportunity. Perhaps your music conveys a subtle message of animal rights. Or maybe the lyrics of your song directly deal with how animals suffer. Either way, you have the chance to reach people. Whether you play at your friend's party or become an international pop star, you can make a difference. It doesn't matter whether you play classical music, sing ballads, or are into hip-hop; there is a place for you.

Vegan Evan (7) of Florida, says, "I like rapping. It's a good way to spread the message about going vegan and what animals go through. It's fun to make people smile and make them think."

Vegan Evan and rapper Grey

WEAR YOUR HEART ON YOUR SLEEVE

You're already avoiding wearing animal skins and fur because of the cruelty, but your clothes can also allow you to spread an animal friendly message in an easy and fun way.

There are loads of awesome shirts, bags, and buttons available with all kinds of messages that could make someone think or even start a conversation. If you can't find anything you like, then you can make your own.

INSPIRATION

Emma Black (14), Wollongong, Australia

"When I first became an activist I bought a shirt which said, Go Vegan, Baby! I wore it around heaps when I was walking. It was a subtle form of activism that I could do whilst I was doing other stuff.

"One day someone came up to me in a café and said they liked my shirt. They asked me if I was vegan, and when I said yes they said, 'Oh, you are so young!' I said, 'You are never too young to make a change to better the world.' That was the start of a conversation with them."

For the extroverts among you who are happy to have conversations with random strangers, an effective shirt message might be Ask Me Why I'm Vegan.

If you're willing to answer the question in a polite and patient way, then this message is a pretty awesome way to get your activism on. It is low cost and low effort, but could have great results.

Some activists choose to get this shirt in lots of different colors and styles and wear it all the time. That way, when they go to the grocer's or the airport or the park, they encourage conversations from people who might be interested. It also saves you approaching people.

Bianca Jade (12) and Kenia (15) of Italy love to start conversations on animal rights by proudly wearing their Ask Me Why I'm Vegan shirts.

Another strong message shirt is the one pictured on the next page from Compassion Company (Compassionco.com). The message that *Humane Meat Does Not Exist* is likely to start some interesting conversations, and, in all honesty, you can't go wrong with a rainbow unicorn. It's important to check out ethical companies like Compassion Co. because they use vegan ink and they don't exploit humans when they make their shirts.

Photo courtesy of Compassion Company

Sometimes, when I am feeling grumpy or sad, I may want to avoid conversations. I will still be vegan, of course, but I may not want to talk to others about it. On those days I keep my message wear subtle, like my shirt that reads, HENS ARE FRIENDS. But some days I feel like I'm in Hero Activist Mode, and I want to let others know what is happening to animals. Vegan and animal rights shirts are a pretty awesome way to do this. There are loads of ethical shirt companies. But if you are a bit short on cash, you can also revamp your old, blank T-shirts and accessories—vegan style!

You can repurpose some of your plain clothing or go on a fun shopping spree at a secondhand shop to find some plain clothing. You can then use fabric paints to create designs with vegan and animal rights messages.

You know what is even more fun than designing or making message wear on your own? Doing it with friends. Making message wear could be a fun project to do with your animal rights team.

Now all you have to do is rock your message wear and get ready to chat if people ask you about it.

Use #SavingAnimals to share your message wear on your socials.

Struggling for a slogan? Answer these questions to find out what kind of message may suit you.

1. Do you like talking to people?
2. Do you like answering questions?
3. Do you feel like you can answer questions about being vegan?

If you answered yes to two or more questions, try out these slogans:

ASK ME WHY I'M VEGAN

NO SUCH THING AS HUMANE MEAT

EATING ANIMALS IS WEIRD

If you answered no to two or more questions, try out these slogans:

PLANT POWERED

FRIENDS, NOT FOOD (with a cute pic of an animal)

LOVE US, DON'T EAT US (with a cute pic of an animal)

Don't be constrained by these questions, though. Create whatever designs you feel inspired to create. Get arty, make a mess, and get your message out there.

Above, young activist **Vegan Evan (7), of Florida**, shows off his LOVE ANIMALS? #GOVEGAN T-shirt.

STICKERING

Stickering is a great way to get people thinking. You can place vegan or animal rights stickers on your schoolbooks, your locker, or around the house. Some stickers are made to be put on the packaging of food items to make people think. The best thing is that stickering is something you can do right now.

Some animal rights organizations will send you free stickers if you ask them. Another option is to buy blank labels and design and print your own stickers. To keep it really simple, you can just write your message on the blank label, and off you go.

For example, you could write, "I wanted to live" and stick that on a chicken body at the supermarket. Or you may prefer to write a fact on your stickers, like "Chickens are killed at only six weeks old." People may not realize they are about to eat a chick.

Zoe Rosenberg (15) of San Luis Obispo, California, sells animal rights stickers in her Etsy shop. Any profits from Zoe's stickers go to help the animals at her sanctuary. Check them out here:

Etsy.com/shop/AnimalRightsEtsy

You can also buy great stickers here:

Etsy.com/au/shop/ActivistStickers

Ateret Goldman (16) of Berkeley, California, says…

> The main reason I think stickering is effective is because it builds an activist identity. Each of us has levels of identity that make us up as a person. For some people, an important part of their identity may be that they're a mom, and that will influence the choices they make. The next most important part of their identity may be that they love soccer, the next is that they love the color pink. All those things will influence their choices. When they are faced with choices, they will make them depending on their priorities.
>
> Every time you go to the gas station or grocery store, wherever there are products of violence towards animals, you are taking action for them. You are spreading awareness saying, "Hey, this is not okay," and putting a sticker down. So when a decision is to be made, you can take your activist identity into account. Maybe once you have built up your activist identity, a protest won't seem so scary.
>
> I have sent thousands of stickers around the world. More people are taking action than ever before. It's easy to be a silent vegan, but if you are taking action every time you go to a grocery store, you are probably more likely to get active in other ways.

As far as outreach, I think even if all it does is make shoppers think for a second, "Oh, that's a weird sticker," it's still good. Currently we live in a world where violence towards animals is normalized, and what we're trying to do is provide resistance towards that. We want to normalize action and justice. Stickering does help with that.

NOTE

Sticker at your own risk. While you can put stickers all over your personal things, shops will not like it if you do it there. Some people say if the food is thrown out after stickering, then that is a waste. But I feel that it was a waste as soon as that animal was made to suffer and die. Stickering could be seen as a form of economic sabotage. If you feel weird about that, you could sticker the shelf below the animal flesh and secretions instead (next to the price labels). Do with this information what you will.

POSTERS

For introverts, some forms of activism may feel a little overwhelming at first. I mean, it may have felt enough of a challenge wearing a message tee out in public. Having a conversation about a controversial subject is a whole other matter.

Don't worry; there is vegan outreach that you can do without having to interact with a single person.

Posters are another way to speak up for animals. You can find notice boards all over the place, like in communities and schools. A lot of boards are open for anyone to post on. You can also post on the back of public toilet doors (people love something to read while on the loo) and on lampposts.

For art and design lovers, this is an opportunity to get creative. But for the time-poor, some activists have already made posters that they are happy to share (it's all for the animals, after all).

Have you seen those posters on which people advertise a service, and you can pull off a tab and get the person's number? Well, these posters are designed the same way, except instead of a phone number it will be a website where people can either watch a video or get more info about becoming vegan and helping animals.

Check out Absolutevegan.org for a huge choice of free posters to print out.

When creating your own posters, you want to keep the message simple and effective. You don't have much space, after all.

You could write …

Be Kind, Be Vegan

Love Animals, Don't Eat Them

Animals Want to Live

Watch *Dominion*

Be One Less Person Hurting Animals — Go Vegan

These posters may not turn someone vegan, but they will plant a seed, and who knows where that will lead?

If you prefer to create your own posters, use the one above for inspiration. Consider using these four elements:

1. Cute photo of an animal
2. Simple slogan
3. Suggested documentaries to watch
4. Tabs with the URL of a website to learn more

CHAPTER 8

EFFECTIVE VEGAN OUTREACH

The most effective activism often involves one-on-one interaction, where you make real connections with individuals.

This kind of sucks if you lack confidence. Some of the young activists I spoke to were very nervous about outreaching at first. But over time, they gained confidence. When you are talking to people, remember ...

If they are angry, they may realize they are doing something wrong.

They may be angry because they know their behavior does not line up with their ethics. They may be angry because they do not want to change. They may be angry because they do not want to learn the truth.

They are not really angry at you (although it may seem like it), so try not to take it personally.

Speaking of anger, you may find yourself feeling angry at people who just don't care about animal suffering. Getting mad at people may feel good at the time, but it rarely helps the animals. I know this from experience, as my natural reaction to cruelty is anger; however, this just makes people shut down.

Be polite and be yourself. If you don't know the answer to a question, just be honest. There is no need to guess what you should say. You know that cruelty and exploitation of animals is wrong.

Remember this: **Animals are not ours to use**. Remember how you wouldn't like to be used against your will and that will help you answer most questions.

If you are outreaching about one specific issue, such as getting rid of hatching projects in schools or a campaign to stop the animal circus coming to town, then spend some time researching the topic online beforehand. Read the leaflets you are giving out. That way, the knowledge will be fresh in your brain.

You can also answer difficult questions by referring people to a helpful website. This may help if you are not sure of a certain topic. For example, if someone asks you a health question and you are not sure of the answer, you could say, "I'm not sure about that. I do this for the animals, but there is a lot more info about being vegan for health at NutritionFacts.org if you want to check it out."

A polite attitude and a friendly smile will get you through most sticky situations. Having said that, there are some questions that activists get asked time and time again. It doesn't hurt to be prepared, so have a read through the questions and answers we talked about in the Family Matters chapter. A lot of the questions your friends and family ask you will be repeated by strangers. (Hey! Dealing with your difficult family was good practice, after all!)

LEAFLETING

Handing out leaflets about going vegan can be an effective way to educate people about what happens to animals. A group called Vegan Outreach (VeganOutreach.org) organizes volunteers to go to college campuses and hand out leaflets to students. The leaflets educate people about speciesism, the use of animals, and how to go vegan. The reason Vegan Outreach focuses on leafleting is because it gets people thinking. It plants seeds of compassion, and it's easy! You can hand out leaflets on your own or in a group, and you can make a real difference for animals.

Emma Black (14) of Wollongong, Australia doing vegan outreach

There are a lot of organizations that have created vegan leaflets. If you send them an email, they may send you some leaflets to hand out. Check out VeganOutreach.org, PETA.org, AnimalsAustralia.org, and VeganEasy.org for a start.

If you are leafleting about a single issue, then you can make your own leaflets. You can stand in a busy pedestrian area or you can drop them in letterboxes door-to-door.

Bailey Mason (16) of Sydney, Australia, regularly holds protests at Dolphin Marine Magic. This is an aquarium that keeps dolphins and other animals captive in small pools. Bailey says leaflets are an important part of his outreach.

BAILEY'S TOP TIPS ON MAKING YOUR OWN LEAFLET

» Research your topic and fact-check everything.
» Write down all the info you can think of on the topic, and then choose the most important points to include on your leaflet.

» Include a photo of an individual animal, as that helps people make a connection. In one of his leaflets, Bailey added a photo of a baby dolphin who had died at Dolphin Marine Magic.

» Use a software program to make the leaflet clear and attractive.

» Print out your leaflets.

» When you hand out your leaflets, listen for feedback and make changes for next time.

A COFFS HARBOUR DOLPHIN IS BEING MISTREATED.

Dolphin Marine Magic's current management is putting **profit above animal welfare**. The facility continues to put Bucky on show and have him give rides to heavy tourists even though **he is elderly and has cancer**. This is **inhumane treatment** of such an intelligent animal. This is outrageous and 200k people have signed a petition demanding the Coffs Harbour facility stop this heartbreaking abuse on Bucky.

Exploiting an elderly dolphin that has cancer and continuing to breed dolphins in tanks is animal cruelty. Please don't buy a ticket.

Leafleting can be a bit scary at first, but it can also be really effective, and once you have handed out your first leaflet, your fears will start to melt away.

Hannah McKay (16), Orange, New South Wales, Australia

When I was fourteen, I ordered leaflets from PETA. Some leaflets were about circuses, some were about dairy, and others about fashion and entertainment. The leaflets showed the truth about what happens to animals in these industries.

I ordered fifty of each leaflet and put one of each in paper bags. Me and my friend made up the leaflet packs and then went door-to-door in our town and gave them out. It was a bit scary, but I felt a lot better after doing it. Even though I live in a rural area where people can be mean to animals, most people calmly took the leaflets. There wasn't any conflict.

ACTIVIST PROFILE

Emi Pizarro Zamora (9), Brisbane, Australia

Nine-year-old Emi is already a regular on the animal rights scene and has been vegan for four years.

Why did you go vegan?

I was raised vegetarian. My family went vegan before me, but it was a personal decision for me. I thought about the animal cruelty in dairy and eggs. It made me sad to think about what was going on in slaughterhouses. I didn't want to support that anymore. I didn't find it hard to change. I guess because I had a lot of support. My friends did ask a lot of questions, but I stayed calm and explained veganism to them. Mostly, they were quite nice about it.

What kind of activism do you like to do for animals?

I love protesting. I speak on the megaphone and tell people what is happening to animals. I usually have someone helping me. When I saw the adults speaking on the megaphone, I wanted a try, and I loved it.

I also like to give out leaflets about going vegan and how to save animals and the environment.

I sometimes do video outreach where we hold TV screens and allow people to see what happens to animals. I either hold the screen or I give out leaflets. People get sad when they see the footage and they realize what is happening to animals.

Do you have any leafleting tips?

Being young makes it easier because I find people are more likely to take the leaflet from me. I guess they don't want to hurt my feelings. I just hold the leaflet out, smile, and say, "Would you like to take this leaflet about helping animals?" If you look friendly, you do better.

Do you find it hard learning about the horrible things that happen to animals?

Sometimes, but I keep focusing on the animals. I imagine the animals walking free from harm once I am finished.

Have you ever been to a farm sanctuary?

I went to Farm Animal Rescue (FarmAnimalRescue.org.au). There were so many gorgeous cows, and I got to pat them. That was my first-ever time to see a real-life cow, and they licked me with their rough tongues. It made me laugh. I was happy to see them free from harm.

How do you think other kids could help animals?

Start with something easy, like making a sign about animal rights and holding it up at a protest. Then try giving out leaflets or holding a TV screen showing what's happening to animals. If you are feeling brave, you could speak on a megaphone. Do your research so you know the facts, and then see how brave you can be.

TABLING

Tabling is a tried-and-true form of activism. With permission, you can set up a table in your town, college campus, or school playground. On that table, you provide people with information about animal rights and going vegan.

Tabling allows you to combine a few methods of activism. It's multitasking for the animals. You can wear your vegan message wear. You can display leaflets on the table. You can bake vegan cupcakes for people to try, and you can even have a laptop or tablet playing videos.

The difference between tabling and leafleting is the table (I know, I'm a genius!). You have one place where people can come and get lots of information. People will be coming to you, so they will already be interested when they come over.

How to attract people to your stall

There is a lot of debate over what is more effective for outreach: graphic images or cute animal pics?

Photo courtesy of Charlize Reynierse

Zoe Rosenberg (15), San Luis Obispo, California

If you are showing people what is happening to animals with leaflets or video footage, I suggest attracting them to your stall with cute animal images. The thing is, we don't have to convince people to love animals; most people already do. We need to tell them how animals are being used, and why mistreating animals because they are another species is wrong. Cupcakes and cute pics will get people to you, and the footage will do the rest.

VIDEO OUTREACH

Video outreach is when activists hold TVs or laptops that are playing footage of what happens to animals on farms and in slaughterhouses. This is like leafleting 2.0 and has become a popular and effective form of activism in recent years.

All you need to do to get started is to download footage of what happens to animals from a site like Farm Transparency Project (FarmTransparency. org) or Mercy for Animals (MercyForAnimals.org) and ensure you have a laptop or other device to show the video. If you are standing in one location, you will probably need to apply for a permit.

Be aware that these videos are quite graphic and may be disturbing.

Even easier than organizing this yourself is to join a group that is already active. One group that runs regular video outreach all around the world is called Anonymous for the Voiceless (AnonymousForTheVoiceless.org). They call the video activism The Cube of Truth (see the photo of Emi Pizarro Zamora above).

People stand back to back in a "cube" with each TV or laptop showing a different form of animal use, including slaughter. There is often emotive music playing. People in the cube usually wear masks so that their faces and expressions don't distract from the video. This gives members of the public the chance to watch without worrying what the activists think of them. Other activists are available to talk to the person watching the video and to give them information about going vegan. The viewer will have a lot to think about after watching the video, and some people go vegan on the spot.

Truth on the move

In Sydney, we have a group called "Truth Walkers." They work a bit like the cube, but they take their TV screens on the move. The large screens are powered by battery packs that can be carried in a backpack. This means the activists can walk down the street or go to any event or disruption with the screens playing footage. What a great opportunity to show members of the public what is happening to animals.

Because the activists are walking around, they don't need to apply for a permit, and if the police give them a move-on order, they simply walk to another location. They can walk past butcher shops and restaurants, through a market, or just around the town. If you don't have TV screens, you can use a laptop. A speaker could also be plugged in and carried along.

Easy steps to get started with video outreach

Perhaps the easiest way to start is to see if there is a video outreach group already in your area. If there isn't a group near you, you could talk to Anonymous for the Voiceless about starting one. It isn't essential to work with an established group, though. You can get started on this with just your friends. Below are a few tips.

1. Choose which video clips you would like to use. Showing footage from your own region is a good idea, as otherwise people might say, "That doesn't happen here."
2. Get some friends together and set a date and location for your outreach. A Facebook event may be helpful.
3. Apply for a permit, or plan to take your activism on the move.
4. Buy or make some masks if you want to use them.
5. Order or make some leaflets about veganism to hand out to people who watch the video.

Some people use video activism in a different way. They may pay people $1 to watch the video, or give them a delicious vegan cupcake in return. Okay, this is bribery—but it's bribery of the very best kind. People get something, and they find out more about animals and how to be kind to them.

In Sydney, there is an activist group called Save Poppy. The founder of Save Poppy, Andy, lets people pat his gorgeous dog Muffin if they watch the video. Talk about motivation!

Priscilla Huynh (20) of Sydney, Australia, uses her baking skills to advocate for animals.

Priscilla says, "Cupcake challenges are one of my favorite types of activism—and from experience, it is effective. This is where you give a cupcake (or any other vegan food) to a person if they watch a short video on the animal agriculture industry. We usually show the four-minute video *Thousand Eyes* by Farm Transparency Project, which can be found on YouTube. It contains a powerful selection of the footage used in the documentary *Dominion*. I believe this is effective, as the participant takes the time to sit down and watch a video they would usually turn away from. This opens their mind and allows them to be more receptive when you explain and answer their questions about the animal agriculture industry. Furthermore, they get to taste delicious vegan food, which breaks the perception that vegan food tastes unpleasant."

Priscilla continues, "At a university cupcake challenge, I spoke to an exchange student who had never seen the footage we showed, and he was shocked by it. He had a lot of questions about health and fitness, as that was his interest area. My friend and I answered his questions politely, and he thanked us for our time and took a leaflet. We exchanged Instagram usernames so he could reach out if he had any more questions. He didn't go vegan straightaway, but after watching *The Game Changers* documentary he reached out to me as he wanted to be vegan. I gave him easy recipe ideas to try, and he has been vegan ever since. He has even become an activist. After a productive outreach conversation, I feel hopeful for the animals, and it drives me to continue speaking up. I call these conversations 'golden conversations,' and this is what excites me most about being an activist."

For **Charlize Reynierse (22) of Sydney, Australia**, her first experience of activism was video activism. "I found out about the first video activism taking place in Sydney. It was organized by Save Poppy [SavePoppy.com]. During the event, I felt so grateful to have somewhere to put my energy. After everything I had learnt about animal agriculture, I was feeling angry. When I first went vegan I really thought when I told my friends and family what was going on they would be as appalled and shocked as I was and would make changes. Instead they became defensive and refused to change. I would lie awake at night thinking: I have this knowledge, I need to do something about it. I didn't know a single other vegan, so it was very new to me. I was introverted and had social anxiety at the time, so it was difficult but also rewarding to connect with like-minded people. By doing the Save Poppy and Cube of Truth events, it helped a lot with my anxiety. I got more used to talking to people. Before the first event I attended, I thought I was just going to hold screens showing the video as I was anxious, but by the end I did outreach some people. I found it hard, but I got better with time. I was surprised to find that I felt energized rather than drained at the end of the event."

Emma Black (14) of Wollongong, Australia, pictured above, also takes part in the Sydney Cube of Truth. "On the first day I was too scared to outreach to anyone, so I stood in the cube the whole time, holding a TV screen with the mask over my face. I was amazed to see people's reactions to the video. Many people had never seen this kind of footage before. I could see their shock and sadness. I saw one lady who was brought to tears.

She was really sad that she had been contributing to the cruelty for so long After that first time, I gave outreach a go. It was scary at first, but the more I do it, the more confident I feel."

Emma's Outreach Tips

» After someone has been watching the footage for a while, I approach them, and if they speak English, I ask them how the footage makes them feel. I may ask if they have seen that kind of footage before.

» Sometimes I will say, "What do you think of animal cruelty?" Most people will say, "It's horrible." Then I ask them whether they think we need to exploit animals. They may say yes and share their beliefs. That is when the conversation really starts. I try to listen carefully and respond to their questions.

» Having a template of what questions to start off with makes it so much less nerve-racking. The more research you do on veganism, the more confident you will feel talking to people. I've done a lot of research, so I feel confident telling people that we can thrive on a vegan diet. I tell them the health benefits as well as how animal agriculture is terrible for the environment and how it hurts animals.

Seven keys to effective video outreach

1. Practice at home by coming up with ideas of how you will start your conversation.
2. Watch videos of people who are really good at outreach, like Earthling Ed on YouTube.
3. Open the conversation with a question like, "What do you think of animal cruelty?"
4. Listen to the person's response.
5. Ask them open ended, non-judgmental questions to find out more about how they are feeling.
6. Relate to them with stories about your own activism: "When I used to eat meat ... "
7. Leave them with a plan for what steps they can take to go vegan. Help them come to a conclusion on their own.

SCREENING FILMS

Documentaries are perhaps the most effective way of helping people learn the truth about animal agriculture and helping them change their behavior to reflect their beliefs. It could be as simple as organizing a meet-up or sleepover with your animal rights group and watching a vegan documentary. Or you may decide to use your school hall or other facility and invite members of the public to come along.

HOW TO ORGANIZE A DOCUMENTARY SCREENING

Choose which film you would like to screen and think about why. Do you think it will help people be kinder to animals?

Choose a venue and book it in. Is it going to be a small screening at your house with your friends? Just make sure your parents know when you need the TV room. Is it going to be a bigger event? See if a community hall or school is available. Sometimes there will be a fee, but hopefully there will be a space in your community for free. Please also note that you may have to pay a fee to the filmmakers if you are hosting a public screening. However, this is money well spent, as it allows the filmmakers to keep doing their good work. And, if you do need to raise money to pay a fee, you might have a vegan bake sale to raise the funds, or sell homemade vegan goodies at the event to recoup your costs.

Make sure the venue has equipment to screen the film, and check to be sure that it works.

Order some vegan leaflets from Vegan Outreach, PETA, Vegan Easy, or another organization, so people can learn how and why to go vegan after the film.

Prepare vegan snacks and have some water available. Can a group of friends bake some vegan cookies or cakes? Give away the yummiest vegan food you can after the film, and be ready to answer any questions.

Invites! If it is a small event, you may just need to ask people to come along. If it is a larger event, you may want to publicize it on your socials. Set up a Facebook event to see how many people will attend. Advertise the film with posters, leaflets, or Facebook ads.

It's film day! If anyone leaves the film because they are sad or overwhelmed, have someone ready to offer support outside. You may also like to have a leaflet on mental health and self-care available.

Give yourself a great big pat on the back. If the event went well, maybe it is a kind of activism you would like to do again in the future.

FILMS TO SCREEN

Be sure to do some research first to check that the film you plan to screen is suitable for the intended age group. Some of the films below may not be suitable for certain age groups due to scenes of animal slaughter.

THE VEGAN MAKERS — ANIMAL RIGHTS

» *Earthlings*
» *Dominion* (Australian animal use)
» *Peaceable Kingdom*
» *Land of Hope & Glory* (UK animal exploitation)
» *Okja* (Fictional story of animal liberation)
» *The Ghosts in Our Machine*

ENVIRONMENT

» *Cowspiracy*
» *A Plastic Ocean*
» *Plastic Paradise*

HEALTH

» *What the Health*
» *Forks over Knives*
» *The Game Changers*

MIXED ISSUES

» *Vegucated*
» *Speciesism*
» Simon Amstell's *Carnage* (comedy)

Hannah Testa (15) of Atlanta, Georgia, at a film screening

YOUTUBE VIDEOS TO WATCH WITH FRIENDS AND FAMILY

Bite Sized Vegan YouTube videos (great for sleepovers)

Dairy is Scary — Erin Janus

The Emotional World of Farmed Animals — Jeffrey Masson

Edgar's Mission Sanctuary Animal Videos

Mic the Vegan

Melanie Joy's speech on carnism

Earthling Ed

Sweet Potato Soul

Cheap Lazy Vegan

Rachel Ama

CHAPTER 9

POWER OF PROTEST

I remember attending my first protest back when I was sixteen years old. A chain of UK hardware stores had made the odd decision to start selling animals, including exotics like snakes and lizards.

My BFF Melissa and I had met a very interesting lady named Hella through our volunteer work at the animal sanctuary. Hella was well known in the local activist scene. She was an aromatherapist with a heavy Dutch accent, a heart of gold, the mouth of a sailor, and absolutely no time for animal exploiters. She had a loud voice, and she was not afraid to use it.

To me, she seemed fearless. Sometimes the sanctuary owner would find anonymously rescued white rabbits waiting for her in the morning. I have a feeling that Hella may have been the one responsible for saving them from a lab. So when Hella asked us to come along to a protest, we jumped at the chance.

The aim of our first protest was clear: to stop the hardware store chain from going ahead with its plan to sell animals. When Melissa and I turned up, I was given white coveralls to change into. I'm still not 100 percent sure of the reason we dressed up in these, but I did as I was told. Hella was the expert, after all.

We then proceeded to hand out leaflets to the public as they entered the shop. The leaflets explained why it was a terrible idea for a DIY store to encourage the impulse buying of animals. Since it was my first time, I remember feeling a bit awkward. I wasn't used to being confrontational, and Hella's style was to get up in people's faces. We got a mixed reception from the public, but the protest got some local media attention, which helped make the community aware of the issue.

Despite my reservations, the protests proved effective, with the chain of stores changing its mind about selling animals. It showed me that protests can be a useful tool for bringing about change.

It is legal to hold a peaceful protest in Australia. You just need to apply for a permit to be in your chosen protest location. Without a permit, you can still protest or disrupt, but you must be prepared to move if you get a move-on order from police. The key to a successful protest is inviting a lot of people and making sure you have a clear ask. If protesting is combined with leafleting or outreach, then even better!

I was inspired when speaking to young activists that so many of them had taken part in or even organized protests.

INSPIRATION

Jasmine Shaw (18), Central Coast, Australia
"I feel strongly that animals should not be used for our entertainment. It's so sad seeing monkeys and lions pacing back and forth at the circus. For a long time I've been signing petitions to send the circus animals to a sanctuary, and I've attended protests. I have always hated the abuse, even when I was little.

"As soon as I found out that the animal circus was coming to my area, I knew that we needed to protest. I got in touch with a local activist who had arranged protests before. She gave me some pointers, and I was able to pull together a well-attended protest. I believe we got a lot of people to think about the cruelty involved in the circus. We got mostly positive feedback from the public."

Steps To Organize a Protest

1. Choose an achievable goal for the protest.
2. Set a date, time, and location for the protest. Make sure the location is safe and in a public place with plenty of foot traffic.
3. Apply for a permit to protest.
4. Create a Facebook event, and share and invite people.
5. Contact local and national animal rights groups and ask them to invite their members to the event.
6. Post regularly on your socials up until the event.
7. Post about the event on local vegan pages and groups.
8. Create bold and bright signs and posters.
9. Decide on chants. Maybe borrow a drum or costumes.
10. Contact the media one week before the event and on the morning of the protest (see page 171 for information on reaching out to the media).
11. Assign one person to talk to the media and one person (a marshal) to organize everyone on the day. The marshal should wear a fluorescent vest.

12. On the day, turn up early with extra signs for other protesters. Arrange to meet everyone fifteen minutes before the event for briefing.
13. If the police turn up, listen to their instructions. They should then let you get on with the protest.
14. Take photos on the day to supply to media and to share on your socials.

Khendall Lil Bear (8) of Florida has taken part in many protests against SeaWorld and the greyhound racing industry. He has also fought to protect Florida's black bears from hunters.

BB, a nine-year-old animal activist from Chile, pictured on the next page, regularly attends vigils, protests, and marches with her mum. "I went to the march against the Chilean rodeo," she says. "Animals can feel. They don't want to be tortured. They want to live. By marching, we are sending a strong message that it is not okay to use and hurt animals at the rodeo. I think marches are a good way to help animals, especially for new activists. You can make signs with your message, for example: SAY NO TO RODEO or STOP ANIMAL CRUELTY."

BE A MEDIA STAR

If you are organizing a protest, disruption, or any other campaign to help animals, you may be able to reach a wider audience with the help of the media. After all, the more people who are aware of your action, the more successful it will be.

You can share the action on your socials and even contact high-profile activists to ask them to share it, but sometimes good old-fashioned local news will get more eyes on your action.

HOW TO WRITE A PRESS RELEASE

A press release is a statement you send out to relevant papers or media outlets to let them know a piece of news. In your case, this could be about your protest or another animal action, like trying to save the ag animals at school or trying to stop a hatching project.

Don't just send out the press release willy-nilly. Do some research to find a local paper that is likely to publish your piece, and look up the editor's email address. You could have a look through papers or online articles to find a journalist who is most likely to write a story on animal rights. Maybe they write about consumer affairs or lifestyle. Write an email to that journalist.

The subject of the email should be the heading of your press release, for example: "Local Teen Protests Cruel Animal Circus."

The body of the email should start with a friendly hello to the journalist: "Dear Ms. Doe, I thought you might be interested in this local story ... "

Next, write the date and location, followed by the story. Use the tips below to help you.

» Try to include quotes from two people and keep it under 300–400 words.
» Write in short paragraphs and easy-to-read sentences.
» Write the release so that it could be published in the local paper as is.
» At the end, include your name and phone number, and thank the journalist for their time.
» Attach a couple of high-quality photos.

On the next page is a press release I wrote after we rescued some dumped chickens from a park. The aim of the press release was to draw attention to the fact that chickens are being dumped on a regular basis and to push the message that chickens are not disposable. You will see how I used the guidelines above. The journalist loved the press release and published the story on the front page of the local paper.

Press Release Example

Have a look at the press release below, with tips in italics.

Hello,

Here is a local story I hope you may be interested in covering:

Urgent Rescue of Dumped Chickens
Dumped Chickens Saved
[Note: Offer two optional headlines.]

May 16, 2018 — Scahill Street, Campsie
[Location and date of release]

Early Wednesday morning, local resident Kirsti Claymore was walking her dog when she happened upon thirteen dumped chickens.
[Try to sum up the story in the opening sentence.]

"I couldn't believe it when I saw the chickens," said Ms. Claymore. "I saw an open guinea pig hutch and twelve chickens roaming around looking scared. My heart broke to see a thirteenth hen dead on the ground. It made me sick that someone had been so cruel. I couldn't just leave them there, so I contacted NSW Hen Rescue and used my local community Facebook group to find more volunteers."
[First quote]

NSW Hen Rescue usually rescues chickens from factory farms, but the vegan volunteer group knew they had to act to help the dumped chickens.

"When we heard one hen was already dead, we had to get over there as soon as possible," said Catherine Kelaher, founder of the rescue. "They were at risk

from predators, and they had no food, so we were pleased a local person cared enough to get in touch with us."
[Second quote]

When the NSW Hen Rescue team arrived, they found Inner West WIRES were already at the scene and had caught most of the chickens.

"It was great teamwork," said Ms. Kelaher. "There was one big, handsome rooster, who we have named Leo, and eleven hens."
[Try to show that the animals are individuals.]

This is a situation NSW Hen Rescue is all too familiar with.

"We are getting a lot of calls about dumped chickens from the South West Sydney area," said Ms. Kelaher. "Many people see chickens as disposable. They breed them or take part in school hatching projects and don't think about what they will do with the roosters. You can't keep roosters in residential areas, so it is irresponsible to bring them into the world. People need to understand that chickens deserve compassion just like dogs or cats and that when you take them on, you take them on for life.

"Chickens are all individuals with likes, dislikes, and different personalities. For example, Leo the rooster is incredibly gentle and sweet with the hens. They deserve care and respect. They deserve not to be exploited."

NSW Hen Rescue is run out of a rented suburban back garden, so Ms. Kelaher has had to get creative using her spare bedroom as a temporary coop until the feathered family can be found a good home.

"We have a vetting system in place," she said. "When a chicken comes into our care, we want to make sure they are safe for life. After everything they've been through, it's important to us to keep this family together. Our motto is: 'Saving one animal may not change the world, but it will change the world for that one animal.'"

To adopt, foster, or donate towards vet bills, go to www.henrescue.org
[Note: End the press release with a call to action. For a protest, you could add the date and time of the protest here.]

Note to Editor:
For more info please contact:
[Add your name, email, and phone number here.]

Please find supporting photos attached.
[Ideally, photos should include at least one of the two or more people quoted. People and animals are perfect.]

Thanks so much for your kind consideration.

NON-VIOLENT DIRECT ACTION

Ateret Goldman (16) of Berkeley, California

Non-violent direct action (NVDA) is a tool that has been utilized in every single social justice movement that has been successful before us. NVDA is the act of going into places that are being violent towards animals or that are normalizing violence towards animals and bringing the truth and bringing love. It is speaking the truth even in the face of persecution, even when our voices are not welcomed, and even when it is uncomfortable.

We know that this animal abuse is a systemic issue, that most of us were once part of it. We don't hate the farm workers. We know that they are trapped in this system that treats animals as property. We are trying to change that. We are speaking up for the animals no matter what.

Non-violent direct action can take many forms. It may involve attending a vigil, taking part in a protest, or disrupting a butcher's shop.

I have been arrested twice for animal rights. I think that doing these compassionate acts ought not to be a crime. We look up to Martin Luther King, Jr. There is this angelic image of him as a law-abiding citizen. In reality, he was arrested many times. He said, "One has a moral responsibility to disobey unjust laws." If we recognize the urgency of the animal rights movement, if we see that the ones we are fighting for do not have legal rights, then of course we are going to break the laws and make the world we want to see happen. I want to create the world I want to live in.

If you think compassion is a crime, let's talk about that.

The first time I was arrested, I was fifteen. I went inside a Whole Foods store and, behind the butcher's counter, I had a funeral for the animals. I put flowers on top of their bodies. This simple action landed me a federal charge: a felony and a misdemeanor. I think it shows the power of disobedience. This five-minute action featured in many press articles. Not only that, but countless activists have got involved in animal rights because they found the action inspirational.

The second time I was arrested was at a pig-roasting festival. The people at this festival believe they have figured out a humane way to kill someone who doesn't want to die, which I find quite mind-boggling. So they are parading around the entire body of a pig and telling people how to cut her apart. It is very disturbing, so we disrupted this event. I was arrested, not for going on stage or anything too radical; I was just filming and documenting what was happening. I was arrested because they are so threatened. I was like, "Hey, I don't want to disrupt your night, but there is a dead body, like, right here. Can we just think about that?" That message is so threatening to companies that exploit animals.

What we face is nothing compared to what the animals are going through. My punishment for the so-called crimes was volunteering, at Happy Hen Animal Sanctuary. I enjoyed every moment of my so-called punishment as it was a chance to spend time with my animal friends.

Ateret was part of the first-ever daylight open rescue in San Francisco in 2017. The photo on the following page shows her holding Tikva (meaning Hope), who was saved just moments before slaughter.

Bailey Mason (16) of Sydney, Australia

Bailey uses all kinds of activist tactics as part of his campaign against Dolphin Marine Magic, a facility which keeps dolphins in small pools for entertainment. A non-violent disruption was one of these actions.

> I decided to do something to show that I would not stand idly by whilst the dolphins at Dolphin Marine Magic were abused. A lot of people couldn't believe I decided to do it. I went inside Dolphin Marine Magic, and, at fourteen years old, I disrupted a dolphin show by myself. I stood up whilst holding up my large poster showing a dolphin in a fishbowl saying, FREEDOM, NOT TANKS.
>
> I chanted, "It's not cute, it's cruel. It's not cute, it's cruel." I walked around saying that with the sign. The show stopped. All eyes were on me and not on the dolphins performing ridiculous tricks. I was surrounded by staff members and dolphin trainers. The staff members were rushing around, not knowing what to do. They had not been expecting it.
>
> Thankfully, I had my mum there, who was protecting me. I

179

was escorted out, but I spoke up for those dolphins, and that was my goal.

I knew it was the right thing to do. I had been nervous about how people would react, but then I heard the dolphin trainer say, "And Bucky is performing." Bucky is an elderly dolphin. He was in remission for cancer. His son, baby Jiji, died in captivity. He swallowed rubbish that had been left in the pool.

I knew forcing Bucky to perform was wrong. So I thought, "I'm doing this for Bucky." My nerves just faded, and I stood up.

Emma Black (14) of Wollongong, Australia, took part in a butcher-shop disruption with a local animal rights group in Sydney. Emma says, "The disruptions I've taken part in have been some of the most empowering moments of my activism journey. They help show the community the harsh injustice involved in their everyday food choices, and it is my way of saying: I won't stand for this. Attending these disruptions is something I would recommend to everyone, no matter their age."

Kevin Courtney Black (22) of California says that "any activism I have ever done has been peaceful, whether it is a protest or helping out with a strike. However, I do understand when others feel that peaceful protests are not enough anymore. I just hope that it never gets to that point with my work. I love animals. I love being vegan, and I love standing up for what is right. All three of these things make me who I am today, and I couldn't be prouder."

Callan Flynn (11) of Sydney, Australia, is passionate about bringing an end to live export. As well as writing letters to members of Parliament, he has also attended protests to speak up for the animals and demand an end to the cruel trade.

VIGILS

Vigils can be confronting and heartbreaking, but I found that many of the young activists I spoke to had taken part in this form of activism.

So what is a vigil?

A vigil is an event in which a group of people gather to peacefully bear witness to animals en route to slaughter. The activists may offer water or comfort to the animals if possible. Or they may simply be there, showing that someone cares about these poor individuals. The activists aim to be a non-violent presence so close to one of the most horrifying places on earth.

BB (9) of Chile (pictured on the next page) says, "I attend vigils a lot. It's where we wait for a truck with animals arriving at the slaughterhouse, for example a truck full of piggies. We give them water and love before they're killed. I think vigils are important because you can give the animals love and you can also teach people about the suffering the animals experience. We share videos and photos so that people see what happens to the animals they eat. They see them broken and scared at the slaughterhouse."

While many groups hold vigils, one organization that you will find all around the world is the Animal Save Movement (TheSaveMovement.org). This is a non-violent organization that encourages others to bear witness in their own community.

At vigils, some people may simply be there to be a compassionate presence for the animals. Others may take live footage or photos to tell these animals' stories.

Oliver Davenport (17) of Melbourne, Australia, says, "I feel taking photos or livestreaming at vigils is a good opportunity to get animals' stories out there. So many people forget what animals are going through at this moment. If I can show an individual animal through my photography; if I can show their fear, their personality, then that means a lot. Social media is a good tool for vigils. Many people livestream. It helps their followers realize that this is urgent. It is confronting for people to see these animals."

Photo by Oliver Davenport

"These cows were so curious," Oliver says of the photo above. "They were terrified, but they still wanted to get a look at what was going on outside. People were looking at them, looking at how cute they were, how beautiful they were. Yet they didn't make the connection that these beautiful souls were going to be murdered just so someone can have a moment's satisfaction of eating their bodies. During the time I spent with them, I was able to apologize for what we humans had done to them and what was going to happen to them. Someday the only place that these animals will have to travel is to sanctuaries, where they will live out their lives without suffering."

Priscilla Huynh (20) of Sydney, Australia, has organized and attended many vigils. Here, she shares her experience.

> No one likes to spend their time standing in front of a slaughterhouse. Attendees don't do this because it's fun; they do this to witness and share the story of victims of the animal agriculture industry. I strongly recommend attending at least one vigil. After attending a vigil, you are able to personally tell

the story of those you have met through your words, photos, and videos. You can share with others what you saw, felt, heard, and smelt. Sharing your firsthand experiences makes your outreaching more powerful. It can also help close friends and family make the connection when they couldn't before.

Vigils affect each person differently. Some activists burn out after attending vigils, and others find the experience motivating. After taking part in a vigil, assess whether or not attending vigils regularly will be manageable for you. If you find that attending makes you feel too sad and overwhelmed, you can always share the photos and social media posts of other attendees, which will help the animals' stories reach a wider audience.

I regularly attend chicken vigils with Sydney Animal Save. They usually start just before midnight and go until 3:00 a.m. It's cold, and there is a lot of waiting. I remember Isy, a fellow Sydney activist, saying that it is cold and wet, but what the animals endure is far worse. I keep this in mind when I go to events and vigils to remind myself of the victims and to stay strong for them.

How to Organize a Vigil

1. Gather a team of trusted and committed people to be organizers with you.
2. As a team, find out the location of a slaughterhouse in your area, when it operates, the entrances and exits, and note any safety issues.
3. Contact the slaughterhouse owner prior to the vigil to explain what you will be doing and ask if the trucks will stop for two minutes to allow you to safely bear witness to the animals.
4. Research to see if you need to apply for a notice of assembly or get other permission to be at the location.
5. Set up an event page and invite people. Ask people to try and bring a non-vegan friend or family member with them.
6. Ensure there are volunteer marshal attendees on the day who wear high-visibility vests and ensure the safety of others. These people

can also offer comfort to others if needed. Witnessing animals going to slaughter can be very emotional.

7. Make sure to have a briefing at the start of the vigil and a debriefing at the end. Ensure there are clear safety guidelines and that no one goes anywhere near the front of the trucks as they sometimes drive very fast.

8. If you need more assistance, contact TheSaveMovement.org for guidance.

Ateret Goldman (16) of Berkeley, California: Vigils should go hand in hand with the sanctuary movement

I have been to quite a few vigils. I find them heartbreaking. But there are benefits of going to a vigil. By being there, by seeing the worst, it is really motivating to do more for the animals.

When you see hundreds of animals being killed over a couple of hours, it establishes urgency. A lot of people don't realize what is happening. Even people who are vegan for the animals don't always realize the urgency as we don't have to see the suffering on a daily basis. But when you see it, it inspires you to fight.

I feel that vigils should go hand in hand with sanctuaries. I know many hens. I've been blessed to get to know them—their personalities, their quirks. So when I go to the vigils and look into the eyes of hens who are destined for slaughter, I see them as my friends. I know their sisters and their brothers. Not only does it make it more powerful, it doesn't make it as hard. It is still completely tragic, but through sanctuaries, I am able to see the future of where our world is headed. In forty years, we won't have to be like this. These animals are going to go from being in these crates, being confined, being killed, to being liberated and being free. It puts things in a different perspective.

The goal of the Save Movement is not just to bear witness. As the movement grows, we won't just be standing there; we will be walking inside the slaughterhouses and taking animals out. We have seen this happen already in Israel and San Francisco. That is why we need to recognize the urgency and help this movement grow.

HOW TO ATTEND A VIGIL

Go to TheSaveMovement.org and search the list of Save groups. If there is not one in your area, you can click on the link to find out how to start a Save group. You may like to go to your first vigil with a trusted friend or family member. Prepare yourself for it to be very confronting, and have a read through our self-care chapter, too.

THINK OUTSIDE THE BOX

Protests don't have to involve chanting on a megaphone. Use your creativity to come up with new ideas.

Oliver Davenport (17) of Melbourne, Australia, says, "I took part in a protest which focused on how lambs suffer. It was called, *Who silenced the lambs*, and it was the most powerful protest I've ever been to. We held up fifteen dead lambs who were found or died in care. Each lamb was held by one person. Between them, they represented the fifteen million lambs who die from exposure each year in Australia. The reason I got into activism was lambs. I saw how they suffer in the winter. How they are born in the freezing cold and how so many die."

"TO MY MIND, THE LIFE OF A LAMB IS NO LESS PRECIOUS THAN THAT OF A HUMAN BEING. THE MORE HELPLESS THE CREATURE, THE MORE THAT IT IS ENTITLED TO PROTECTION BY MAN FROM THE CRUELTY OF MAN." —MAHATMA GANDHI

"There was music, and as I watched I could see members of the public crying. It was so much harder for people to be angry. They were stopped in their tracks. They were upset." — Oliver Davenport

CHAPTER 10

PUTTING THE FUN IN FUNDRAISING

At NSW Hen Rescue, we always have vet bills and animal care costs. Sometimes it feels like we will never have enough money. When someone gives a donation or holds a fundraising event for us, it can provide us with huge relief and allow us to pay off our vet bills.

We know that each time we go and liberate twenty hens from a factory farm, there will be one or two girls who need vet treatment. So we have to make sure we have budgeted for that. If you hold a fundraiser for a rescue or sanctuary, you could help them provide for the animals they have—and you can literally help them save more animals.

You could also raise funds for a vegan outreach charity. Video outreach groups need money for equipment and running costs. Vegan Outreach needs money for more leaflets. Imagine if the money you donate helps create a new vegan. Think of the potential for animals spared.

I remember one of my first fundraising experiences. I was dressed in a giant bunny mascot suit, hopping up and down outside the supermarket in town. My BFF Melissa and I were raising money for our local animal sanctuary. We had collection tins that filled up surprisingly quickly. Melissa had a basket of sweets for kids, and they loved to run up and cuddle the big bunny (me). It was a fun and simple way to raise some much-needed funds for the animals.

Sometimes people feel that donating is a cop-out and not truly taking action for animals, but funds can go a long way toward making the world a kinder place for animals. Every little bit helps, so a small donation from your pocket money or part-time job could make a difference. But if you are strapped for cash, why not organize a fundraiser and get more people involved? It can even be an opportunity for outreach.

Morgan (10) and Danielle (12) Greenfield of New York set up a lemonade stand to raise money for a local dog shelter. Hey, sometimes the old ideas are the best! They also sold vegan cookies. Not only did they make some dogs happy with the dog treats they bought with the funds, but they also showed people how delish vegan cookies are. Win-win!

Fundraising doesn't always mean organizing an event. It can be as simple as dressing up as Batman and hitting the streets with a collection tin, as **Jack Upperton (7)** did. As you can see in this photo, Jack's mum joined him—and yes, she's dressed as a giant chicken. I think she rocks the look! The duo collected money for a New Zealand animal rights organization, SAFE.

If you want to raise money for an organization, it is important that you get written permission on their letterhead. Just send the org an email and explain what you would like to do to raise money for them. You can then print out their letter and take it with you in case anyone asks for proof that you are a legitimate fundraiser. This also gives the organization a chance to help you out in your efforts. They may have donation cans, costumes, leaflets, or posters you can use.

FUNDRAISING IDEAS

Get your thinking cap on and come up with ways to help your favorite charities. Here are some ideas to get you started …

Raffle—Ask people and businesses to donate vegan goodies, sell tickets, set a date for the raffle, and then pick a winning ticket.

Garage sale—Collect your friends' old stuff and get selling.

Sponsored event—A walk, run, silence, bike ride, danceathon, head-shave (your parents will hate that I suggested that one). The only limit is your imagination.

Movie screening—Sell tickets and vegan snacks.

Used book drive—Collect and sell your friends' old books.

Collect "wish list" items—Ask the charity what they need and collect donated items rather than money.

Fundraising bracelets—Make and sell bracelets.

Crowdfunding—Hold an online crowd-funder using a site like GoFundMe.

Make and sell holiday or other greeting cards.

Vegan BBQ—Combine with leaflets for some great outreach.

Collection tins—Dress up in a costume and take donation boxes to the streets.

Talent show—Charge a small fee to attend and sell vegan snacks.

Vegan bake sale—Baking is fun, and vegan cakes and cookies are delicious. Plus, the great thing about vegan baking is that you can lick the bowl clean with no fear of getting sick: no eggs, so no salmonella. Baking lots of goodies with your friends and then selling them is a great way to raise funds and advocate veganism. You can even have some leaflets about animal rights on the table along with vegan recipes and some info about the organization you are raising money for.

HOW TO HOLD A VEGAN BAKE SALE

Since a vegan bake sale is such a great fundraiser, let's look at how you can organize one.

1. Choose which charity you want to raise funds for, and contact them to let them know about the bake sale.
2. Choose some delicious vegan cake recipes (sounds like a good excuse for taste testing). You can find loads online, or buy an awesome book like *Vegan Cupcakes Take Over the World*.
3. Post on your socials, and ask your friends or animal rights group if they will help bake. Find out who is bringing what goodies so you don't double up. Feel free to add some vegan savory items, too.
4. Choose a date for the bake sale and get permission to hold it in the venue. This may be in your school, in your town, or in a local shop. The best venues are places with lots of foot traffic.
5. A week or so out, make a poster or flyers to tell people what's happening. You want to make sure your friends bring money on the day.
6. Post about the bake sale on your socials.
7. Decide on the price of your baked goods, and post a price list.
8. On the day, check that you have a table, tablecloth, plates for the cakes, napkins, and tongs to pick up cakes so you don't have to

use your fingers. For larger bake sales, you may also want some paper bags or boxes so people can take cakes away. Avoid single-use plastic or other unnecessary waste.

9. Consider offering drinks, too, like homemade lemonade.

10. Bring change so people don't have to pay you in exact money.

11. Get selling! You can place a donation box on the table if people want to donate extra to the cause. Cute pics of the animals you are helping and info about the charity will help, too.

12. Pro tip: Put out the vegan recipe for each item you're selling. People may want to know the ingredients—plus you are showing people how easy and delicious vegan baking can be.

13. Count up your money and give it to the charity. Share how much you raised so everyone can join in on the celebration.

Delicious vegan cupcakes baked by Priscilla Huynh @Cakenection

INSPIRATION

Hannah Testa (15) of Atlanta, Georgia, held her first fundraiser when she was only ten years old.

There was a horse sanctuary about twenty minutes from my house. No one really knew about it in my community. I wanted to spread the word about them as the horses there had such tragic stories.

A lot of the girls in my year loved horses, so I knew they would be keen to help raise funds. I decided to hold a movie night where all the girls in my class could watch a movie together. There was an entry fee, which is how we raised the money.

My mom told me on the morning of the event, "It's okay if only a small number of people turn up and you make $100. It's still a huge success. It's $100 more than the horse sanctuary had yesterday."

But we were in for a big shock. Around 300 people showed up, and we raised $2,400 for the horse sanctuary that night. The event even got covered on CBS News. We had a concession stand selling popcorn and cookies. To top it all off, an anonymous donor donated $10,000 the next day after watching the news story.

Wow! Imagine the difference those funds made to the horse rescue. Hannah didn't stop there. She went on to raise funds for other organizations that are helping animals and the environment.

Two years ago, I did some fundraising for the David Sheldrick Wildlife Trust in Kenya. They raise orphan elephants who are lost from their herd or whose parents have been killed by poachers. Poaching is a huge problem in Kenya right now.

There is a shop in our area whose logo is an elephant. I thought it was worth a shot, so I approached them to see if they wanted to help the elephants in Kenya. The owner of the shop loved the idea.

The store agreed to give a percentage of their profit to the elephants every time they sold something with an elephant print.

I also made homemade elephant-shaped cookies. We stayed up late making batches in the hundreds. It was so tiring but so worth it. We ended up raising a lot for the elephants.

HANNAH'S FUNDRAISING TIPS

Be creative. The more original and fun your idea, the more likely you are to get media attention and raise more funds.

Tell the world. Make sure you spread the word about your fundraiser. Share it on your socials, put posters up around your school, and email a press release to the papers. Once you have sent an email, call the media outlets and follow up.

Just ask. Don't be afraid to ask shops and businesses to support your cause. The worst they can do is say no.

Get help. The more people you have to help you, the more funds you can raise and the more fun you will have. Ask your friends, family, and your animal rights club. They may also have some fresh fundraising ideas that you hadn't thought of yet.

Make a checklist. Make a list of everything you need to do before the event to help you stay organized.

CHAPTER 11

COMPANION ANIMALS—A KID'S BEST FRIEND

Non-human animals can be the very best of friends to humans, but humans aren't always very good friends to non-human animals. Even when humans try to provide a good home, they can sometimes struggle to provide a happy, fulfilling life for the animal. In this chapter, let's look at how to give our companion animals the best life possible.

My very first "pet" was Squeaker the guinea pig. I was two years old, and I have vague memories of sitting in a big armchair, holding Squeaker gently on my lap. I remember my older sister, Amanda, had a bunny called Flopsy who lived in a hutch with Squeaker and used to nibble his ears. I remember worrying about this. I felt devastated when Squeaker passed away.

My story is quite typical of young children. We have a natural tendency to love animals, but without proper guidance, we can end up doing more harm than good. Now I care for four guinea pigs who have been rescued from a lab where they were going to be tested on.

Their names are Elvis, Piper, Pudding (who is pictured on the next page), and Esther. I don't call them pets; I call them companion animals, as it feels more respectful. They are not my little pets. They are my friends who are individuals with their own likes and dislikes.

There are so many things I did wrong with Squeaker. I expect he was bought from a pet shop—a place where animals are sold for profit without much regard for their health or the kind of home they will end up in.

Squeaker was kept with Flopsy the bunny. They were not suitable companions for one another. Flopsy bullied Squeaker. My family should have been on the lookout for any bullying and kept each of them with friends of their own species.

Squeaker and Flopsy were kept in a hutch. How boring! They were outside in cold English winters and only brought in for cuddles from an over-enthusiastic toddler and her boisterous older sister.

Now I spend time thinking of ways I can make the lives of my companion animals better. Even now, I am thinking of ways to improve their lives.

Your dog probably thinks you are the greatest person in the world, but do you act like it? Could you take him for more walks? When you do walk him, do you rush him? Or do you give him a chance to sniff all the messages from his doggy friends? Could you get down on his level and play? What does he do when you are at school?

Sometimes people are very excited about adopting dogs at first, but when the excitement wears off, the poor dogs find themselves in kennels, out in the cold or heat, without any attention at all.

HOW WE TALK ABOUT ANIMALS

Language affects how people see the world. When we call animals *it*, we reinforce the idea that animals are objects. Try to refer to animals as *he, she,* or *they* whenever possible. If you don't know their sex, go for *they* until you find out. It is a subtle form of activism. At NSW Hen Rescue, we make sure we give every single chicken a name that suits his or her personality. They are all individuals.

When we say we "own" a "pet," it implies that the animal is a mere object. The truth is, "pets" should be a part of the family, so the term *companion animal, family member,* or *friend* is more respectful. Okay, so maybe your cats won't be offended when you call them pets, but how you talk can help others view animals as individuals.

ADOPT, DON'T SHOP

"You should adopt animals instead of buying them in pet shops," **Morgan Greenfield (10) of New York** says. "Animals end up in shelters every year because they don't have homes. If they are not adopted, they are killed. It's horrible and it's not fair, but it will keep happening as long as people keep buying animals from breeders and pet shops."

Shelters are overflowing with dogs, cats, rabbits, chickens, birds, and guinea pigs. Pretty much every animal people can buy at a pet shop or breeder, people can also dump. At NSW Hen Rescue, we get contacted about dumped chickens every week.

There are all kinds of reasons animals end up in pounds and on the destroy list.

» People don't think through the commitment before buying an animal. They lose interest over time.
» The animal needs vet care, and the carer doesn't have enough money to pay.
» A baby animal grows into an animal not suited to the environment, e.g., a fluffy chick grows into a crowing rooster.
» Someone moves away and they can't or don't want to take their animal family with them.
» Animals are seized after cruelty complaints.
» Someone does not spay or neuter their animals and ends up with unwanted babies whom they struggle to rehome.

Pet shops that sell animals are horrible places. They buy animals from breeders who often keep them in factory farm–like conditions. When activists investigate these places, the conditions they find are much like any other factory farm: concrete pens, overcrowding, untreated diseases, and sad mothers who have had too many litters of puppies and had all of them ripped away. Why? All because some people insist on buying a "designer" puppy.

Pet shops sell "designer" puppies—breeds of dogs who have been selectively bred over many generations to have certain traits. Pugs may be adorable, but they have been bred so that their noses are flat. This makes it really difficult for them to breathe, especially if they are overweight. If someone wants to adopt a certain breed, they should look for a rescue that helps that particular breed (e.g., a pug rescue).

Even if the pet shop was buying animals from a breeder that "looked after" the animals, there is still a massive problem. This is because the animals are still being exploited just because people want to "own" cute "pets." Many of these animals end up in unsuitable homes. I have seen a lot of dogs chained in yards, barking their heads off. Imagine living your life on a chain every single day. Cats, guinea pigs, mice, rats, and birds are also bred in horrible conditions and sold to whoever will pay up.

People often give in to impulse buying when they walk past a pet shop. There's no denying that the animals inside are adorable. They all deserve a good home—of course they do—but the problem is when people buy them, they are funding the pet industry. It is common for people to regret the purchase of the animal. After a couple of weeks, the puppy is still not toilet trained and the family realizes they will be stuck with him for another seventeen years. They shove him in the garden, where he barks, desperate to be part of the pack again, and the humans wonder why they have a badly behaved dog. They may end up giving him to a shelter or dumping him on the street. Can you imagine doing that to a gorgeous dog like Charlie, pictured below having fun on the beach?

ANIMAL ACTION

If you and your family are thinking of adopting an animal, be sure to do your research first. Check how much time and money the animal will need. Research ways you will be able to make their lives as interesting as possible. Is it best to adopt one animal of that species? Or will they need a friend? Come up with a list of shelters in your area to contact. While all the animals at a shelter need help, your family may want to create a shortlist of personality traits you'd like your new friend to have. Maybe they need to be good with other animals or young children. Maybe your family loves walking, so a dog who loves exercise would be perfect. Whoever is your perfect match, you can be sure there is a friend in a shelter waiting to be loved by you.

SPAY AND NEUTER

What about if you already live with a dog or cat? You love that animal, and you think it would be nice for them to have a litter of puppies or kittens. After all, there is no one more adorable than a puppy or kitten, right?

Okay, I agree with you about how adorable baby animals are, but if you want to spend time with them, go and volunteer at a shelter. It's not just adult animals whom people throw away.

Giving a dog, cat, or other companion animal a chance to have a litter of babies is not a good idea. Imagine how many more unwanted animals would be in the world if everyone did that. Not to mention that every time someone rehomes one of the puppies they purposefully breed, a shelter dog loses a chance to find a home.

Whether by accident or on purpose, when people let animals breed, there are always animals that end up dying. For a very short time I worked at an RSPCA animal shelter. A man brought in three baby bunnies. They were adorable. His rabbits had mated "by mistake" and had babies, but he had given the babies a good life so far and regretted the fact that the bunnies had been allowed to breed. Now he hoped the RSPCA would find a loving home for them.

I was on the reception desk, and I told my boss about the new animals.

She asked me to choose which color bunny was cutest, and the others would be killed. That is how it works. If there are too many of a particular breed of dog or other animal, they will be destroyed. What a horrible situation.

Don't worry! In that case, I managed to convince my boss to keep all three baby bunnies, but I lost my job in the process.

While no-kill shelters are overflowing, most animals will end up at kill shelters, and you simply can't trust them to do the best thing for the animals. That is why spaying and neutering is so important.

TRAP, NEUTER, RELEASE

Cats breed in huge numbers. In kitten season, rescue groups are overrun with unwanted and dumped kittens. Lily, the kitten who appears in the photo on the following page, is one of the lucky ones who was rescued from the pound.

Some cats end up on the streets and are called *community* or *colony cats*. Some people call them *feral*, but I don't use that word as it seems disrespectful. After all, when you call someone feral it is not usually a compliment.

There are volunteer groups that feed these cats to ensure they are healthy and to stop them from killing wildlife. They also trap and spay/neuter the cats to ensure they do not continue to breed. Kittens may be rehomed, but older, wilder cats may be released back. Communities have had great success with this in the past.

"ONE CAT JUST LEADS TO ANOTHER." – ERNEST HEMINGWAY

If you want to help your local community cats, do some research online to see if you can find a local group dedicated to feeding them and trapping, fixing, and releasing them. If there is a group, contact them to ask if you can get added to the feeding roster. If there isn't a group for your local community cats, maybe you could set one up? Contact the World League for the Protection of Animals for advice (WLPA.org), and visit Alley Cat Allies (AlleyCat.org).

THE SAD LIFE OF A CAPTIVE FISH

Have you noticed that even pet supply shops that only sell rescued mammals and birds for ethical reasons still sell fishes? Just because fishes are different from us does not give us an excuse to mistreat them.

Siamese fighting fishes (a.k.a., betta fishes) are beautiful and intelligent. Their delicate fins fan out and show off their bright colors. They are known to be territorial and are likely to feel stressed in unsuitable environments. If you care for other fishes, you must ensure you have an extremely large tank so different territories can be established. In pet shops, betta fishes are kept in tanks the size of a drinking glass. The fishes kept in these jars have limp fins and tails and appear depressed.

Maybe people think it's okay to keep fishes in tanks because of the old myth that goldfishes have a three-second memory. I mean, if the tank was a whole new world every three seconds, maybe it wouldn't be so bad. But that is simply not true. Research has shown that fishes have a memory of at least five months. They can even learn commands. As researcher Dr. Mike Webster told the *Daily Mail*, "A lot of people have the image of a goldfish with a three-second memory—and that's not the case at all. There is a lot of evidence now that fish are just as intelligent as many birds and mammals. Many fishes—such as minnows, sticklebacks, and guppies—are capable of the same intellectual feats as, for example, rats or mice. They can learn their way around mazes, they can learn to recognize other fish, and they can remember which individuals are better competitors."

ANIMAL ACTION

Do you already keep fishes in a tank? Do some research and make it your mission to enrich their lives. Could you get a bigger tank and add interesting rocks or plants for them to hide in?

Does a pet store near you sell Siamese fighting fishes? Start a campaign to get them to stop.

CAGED BIRDS

One of the saddest sights is a bird in a cage. When I was living on the Central Coast of Australia, in nearly every other garden I walked past I saw a cockatoo, a galah, or a cockatiel in a small cage. The cages were hung up outside the house as if the birds were mere ornaments. The birds could see the wild birds fly up above, but they couldn't even stretch their wings. Sometimes I would see the wild birds come and visit the caged birds. They would hang onto the side of the cage and talk to them.

Growing up, I had a companion budgie named Peter. He was the most gorgeous boy. He was turquoise with a yellow head. He lived in a cage on the windowsill. I wonder now what it must have been like for him, looking out to the garden while stuck in that prison. We made some effort to enrich his life. I would use my fingers to play "football" with him on the top of his cage with his favorite jingle bell ball. Despite those fond memories, the sad fact is that Peter spent most of his time in the cage, and that was not kind.

If you go past a garden where the people keep a bird in a cage, drop a leaflet in about how to enrich a companion bird's life.

"No beauty in stolen freedom … He wanted his friends." — Oliver Davenport

COMPANION CHICKENS

A lot of people buy hens from breeders, hatcheries, and pet shops. Do you want to know why? Eggs.

Yup, people want to exploit these ladies for their reproductive system. At NSW Hen Rescue, we get contacted daily by people who want to surrender their chickens for all kinds of reasons. Maybe it's because they no longer lay eggs, because they have a health problem, or because the humans just can't be bothered to care for the chickens anymore.

That is why when we rehome rescued chickens, we make sure people complete an adoption application form first and provide us with photos of where the girls will live. People who adopt do so because they want to help the hens, not because they want to exploit them. In fact, we suggest adopters feed the eggs back to the hens. It helps give them a boost as they lose so many nutrients from laying.

As with all companion animals, it is important we look at the chickens' environment to see if it is good enough. Do the chickens have plenty of room to roam and explore? Are there areas for them to dig and play? Are they safe from predators?

One of the most calming things you can do is to sit with chickens or your other animal friends. I lie down on a towel on the grass, and my sweet feathered family comes and hops on me and preens me. It is a joy. I know each member of my special needs flock by name. I know their individual personalities, their likes, and their dislikes.

One of those chickens is my cuddle chicken, Maddie. Three years ago she fell off a truck and ruptured her inner ear. Goodness knows what horrible place she was going to, but she found herself at the edge of a terrifying motorway. Luckily, a fellow activist saved her and drove her to me. I took her to the vet straightaway. Her treatment was intense. For two years, I had to give Maddie all her water by hand. Despite this, she has had a great life so far. She adores dust bathing, lying in the sunshine, and preening her friends. She loves cuddles. I think animals should only be cuddled on their terms. Just like humans, some animals don't want to be touched. Last year, Maddie surprised me by learning how to drink on her own. But we still have a cuddle every single night, and she still sleeps in the house.

As you can see in the photo on the following page, Maddie has a cozy spot in our home, where she waits for her cuddle time.

ANIMAL ACTION

If you have a companion animal, sit with them. Stroke your dog; sit with your chickens or rabbits. Don't grab at them. Let them come to you. Animals don't have to be cuddly or cute to deserve our respect.

BRING DOGS INSIDE

For the brief time I worked at a branch of the RSPCA, I was amazed by how many dogs were found stray during and after a storm. Katrina Webb of the RSPCA told reporter Kirsten Veness in an ABC news report, "They just hear a noise, they start seeing lots of changes in the environment, and they panic." (See the For More Information section for a link to the full story.)

The RSPCA advises people to get their dogs microchipped, which makes it easier to get dogs back home when bad weather scares animals out of their normal comfort zones. That's all very well—and yes, they should be microchipped—but how about suggesting that people bring their dogs inside rather than leave them out in a storm?

Dogs become frightened and escape through fences, but they will not escape from inside the house, especially if they have the comfort of their humans. One thing that surprised me when I moved to Australia was how many people kept their dogs outside at all times, with very little human interaction.

I don't remember every dog's name from my short time at the RSPCA, but one dog, Jess, sticks in my head. She was the sweetest little whippet, the kind of dog who melts when you pat her. After a storm, she ended up at the RSPCA shelter for the third time. When her human came to the shelter, she said there was just no way she could keep her in the yard; little Jess would always escape. She said she had even tried chaining her up in the yard, and Jess had broken free. The woman decided to surrender Jess. She filled in the paperwork, all the while weeping crocodile tears, and Jess was put in a kennel. I hoped she would get a great home with someone who didn't keep her in a yard all day.

I had the next day off work, and when I came back in, I found out Jess had been killed (or *destroyed*, as it says in the RSPCA paperwork). The reason the RSPCA said they could not try to rehome her was because "she would always be an escape artist." This is their attitude for all dogs who jump fences even once or escape one too many times.

I was upset and angry. After all, if the little dog had been brought inside the house during the storm, she would not have escaped. If the "owner" had spent just a little time with her, her death could have been avoided. If the RSPCA had taken the time to think it through, they would realize that with a safe, inside home, Jess would not be able to escape and would have a much happier life. Instead, they chose to kill her.

What is the point of having a dog as a companion if they are just outside barking and trying to escape all the time?

INSPIRATION

Grandpa Dave taught **Morgan (10) and Danielle (12) Greenfield of New York** to do one kind thing every day. Well, the girls certainly ran with that idea. They started Grandpa Dave's Creature Comforts.

Danielle says, "It's a charity where we collect linen, blankets, and towels and bring them to shelter animals to give them comfort. The animals are cooped up in cages all day long. I feel bad for them. I just want them to feel as comfortable as possible whilst they are there."

"We make cat toys and rope chew toys for the dogs," Morgan says. "New York City, where we live, doesn't have a good shelter system, so we are just trying to provide some comfort for the animals. We hate pet shops. When I go past my local pet shop I chant, 'Adopt, don't shop.' Sometimes I will stand outside the pet shop and have a really long conversation about how bad pet shops are and how animals are being killed in shelters. Me and Mom will talk really loudly so the pet shop customers hear us. By adopting, you are saving an animal. It makes a difference. But by buying from a pet shop or breeder, you're adding to the problem. You are contributing to the puppy mill industry. Adopting saves lives."

Morgan continues, "We do this thing called Pillows for Paws Junior. All our friends come over, and we pair up and see who can make the most catnip pillows. Whoever wins gets to pick a prize from the prize box. It's really fun. You get to spend time with people who care about animals, have fun, and make things to give to the animals. It's fun and easy." The girls then take the collected items to the shelter.

"When we drop items off it's bittersweet," Danielle says. "I know we're doing something good. At the same time I feel bad for the animals. It is sad they have been dumped."

The girls also help their family foster dogs. Fostering is where you care for a rescued animal until they find their forever home. It gives the animal a home environment rather than a shelter.

"We have fostered dogs and kittens," says Morgan. "One dog we fostered was called Marzi. She was from Egypt, where she was shot in the eye. She found her forever home. It was sad to say goodbye, but I'm glad we were able to help her. Even after everything she had been through, she was still friendly."

Danielle has helped her mum with charity work in Honduras. "I saw some kids using the dogs for target practice, so I fed the dogs in front of them. I showed them I was being kind to the dogs. I wanted to set a good example. That's what I try to do in my hometown, too. My friends may not go vegan straightaway, but it's about educating other people. They come to our Pillows for Paws events, and at least they are learning and helping animals."

Morgan and Danielle delivering blankets to their local animal shelter

CHARLIE

Just after I moved to Australia from the UK, I adopted Charlie the dog. I took him to the groomer. I had him neutered and vaccinated. I house-trained him so he didn't pee everywhere. I started taking him on walks and got him used to his lead. I remember the first time he bounded across the park. I remember the first time he went to the beach and the first time he swam in a lake next to the ducks.

Charlie had many firsts with me. Now he is sixteen years old. You should always be careful introducing small animals to dogs, but Charlie is such a softy. He has helped me look after guinea pigs, rabbits, piglets (in the photo below, Charlie greets Blue the piglet), cats, and his absolute favorite—ducklings! Charlie just loves ducklings. We once rescued some ducklings from a factory farm. Charlie was very concerned about them. They had their first swim in a baking tray, and Charlie watched on. When one duckling waddled off across the lounge, Charlie followed him to see if he was okay and rounded him up back to the group.

The thing is, when an animal is a true companion like Charlie, a true family member like Maddie, you get so much more from the relationship. You are not using the animal for what they can give you. I can't see any benefit from using animals as ornaments or egg-laying machines or a slight distraction from everyday life.

COMPANION ANIMAL HAPPINESS CHECK

Work through the questions below for each of your animal friends. It will help you find ways to enrich their lives and make them happier.

Does the animal have a healthy diet? Research the optimum diet for the species, and see if you can improve your companion's diet or add variety.

Does the animal have company of the same species? Would they benefit from a companion?

Is the animal healthy? Are they due for a dental check? Worming? Flea treatment? Do they need a nail trim?

Does the animal have enough space compared to their natural environment? Could you give them more space to explore? Think of ways to make the animal's enclosure replicate the best bits of their natural environment. Google search for ideas.

Is the animal safe from predators?

Is the animal protected from heat stress, cold, and the elements?

Is the animal getting enough exercise? Is the exercise fun and interesting for them?

What does your animal friend do when you are not around?

Do they have toys or other enrichment? Look on Pinterest to find ideas.

Are they clean and groomed? Do they have any matts or tangles?

Does the animal have their own space? Is there somewhere to relax and get away from humans?

How much time do you spend with your animal friend, either sitting with them or playing with or walking them?

If you were living the life your animal friend is living, how would you feel? What changes would you like?

By this point you should have lots of thoughts on how to make your animal friends happier. Have fun trying them out.

Ratty exploring Catherine's backpack

CHAPTER 12

SAVING WILD ANIMALS

We are so lucky to share this earth with all kinds of animals. Looking outside into my garden, I will see my beautiful chicken friends, crested doves with their pointy head feathers, pigeons with their petrol-puddle sheen, and rainbow lorikeets so colorful and loud. At night I hear fruit bats squeaking and see their silhouettes against the sky as they fly from tree to tree. I may even be lucky enough to spot a ringtail possum walking along the power lines.

Everywhere we go, we will see different animals. It's so exciting! When I drive out into the bush and spot a mob of kangaroos, I feel like the luckiest person in the world. It feels like I've won a prize.

Yet wild animals are in desperate need of our help. I bet you love watching animals, but not everyone has the same respect for them.

TOO MANY PEOPLE

They say rabbits breed fast, but take a look at humans! According to the Population Reference Bureau, 228,000 additional babies are born into the world every single day. That's on top of the babies that replace all the people who pass away. Not only does this mean that a whole lot more farmed animals will suffer and die for the new non-vegan people, but wild animals also suffer. All those extra people need houses, cars, and resources. The land, materials, and resources they will consume take up space from our wild neighbors.

Take a look around your town. How much space is there for wild animals? Sure, you may see squirrels, possums, rabbits, and foxes sometimes, but imagine how much space they used to have. Your house, all the fields, the ocean … it was all theirs! Humans were just another animal, not taking up all this space with roads, shopping centers, and massive housing developments.

Wild animals are forced to live in proximity to humans, and this causes them to suffer. Whether the animals are killed on the road, entangled in fishing lines or other plastic waste, or whether they have nowhere to live because of deforestation, wild animals are suffering—and it is up to us to make things easier for them in any way we can.

DEFORESTATION

The leading cause of rainforest destruction is animal agriculture. About one acre of lush rainforest is cleared every second. Mostly this land is used to graze cattle or to grow feed such as grains or soy for farmed animals. Being vegan is a strong way to stand up for the rainforests.

In addition to being vegan, many people choose to avoid buying products that contain palm oil. But what's the problem? After all, isn't palm oil a plant food?

Yes, but palm oil plantations are also a cause of mass deforestation. Eighty-five percent of palm oil is exported from Indonesia and Malaysia. Greedy humans know they can profit from palm oil, so they clear rainforest for new palm oil plantations. These rainforests are essential habitat for 300,000 different species of animals. One of those species is the orangutan.

These incredible primates have had 90 percent of their habitat destroyed in the last twenty years. Imagine how you would feel if your home was burned down and destroyed.

When orangutans flee their burning homes, they run toward the towns, where they are met with more violence.

We must say no to palm oil in an effort to save our life-supporting rainforests and the precious orangutans.

Luckily, some amazing sanctuaries are working hard to help orphaned and injured orangutans. But they are up against a lot and need all the help they can get. Find out more at Orangutan.org.au.

WILD ANIMAL RESCUE

If you want to help wild animals directly, a great way to do so is to train as a wildlife rescuer. This will give you the skills to nurse and care for animals who have been injured or displaced, until they are well enough to be released back into the wild.

Gemma Krogh (13) of Gosford, New South Wales, Australia, went vegan after reading *Amanda the Teen Activist*. But she was busy saving animals long before that.

> I had a website called Save Our Wildlife, about all different kinds of wild animals. I put up news stories, my poems, and other articles that will help people find compassion for wild animals.
>
> I keep a rescue kit so that I am always ready to save animals if there is an emergency situation. I would recommend this to other kids. Even if you are not a trained wildlife carer, it's a great idea to ask your parents to keep a rescue kit in the car and at home, so that if you find an animal in need, you can rush them to the vet where wildlife carers can take over.
>
> I'm a junior member of Wildlife Arc (Wildlife-arc.org.au). I've helped care for quite a few wild animals, including turtles, a water dragon, and a blue-tongued lizard. To be a junior member you have to work with a parent or helper. My dad has joined, so we care for the animals together.
>
> Once, we cared for two little orphaned turtles who were left homeless after their dam had been drained. We had to keep them in a large tank and ensure they had the best living conditions. We had to feed them the right food, and when

they were healthy, they were released into the wild.

When I am older I would like to run an animal sanctuary for wild animals. Kangaroos, wombats, and possums sometimes get caught on fences, in bush fires, or are hurt on the road. They need animal sanctuaries to take them in and care for them.

ANIMAL ACTION

In hot weather, leave out shallow dishes of water for wildlife. Be sure to prop a stick in the bowl to help insects get in and out safely.

ANIMAL RESCUE KIT

This rescue kit is inspired by Gemma and includes a few extra items to make this kit handy if you find a stray dog or cat, or a chicken who has fallen from a truck.

"When you have an injured or distressed animal it is best not to handle her much," Gemma says. "Keep her in a dark and dry place. If you find a dead animal on the side of the road ask your guardian to move the body off the road. This will help protect crows and other scavengers who may pick at the carcass, putting themselves in danger of cars. If the animal has a pouch, gently feel it. There may be a baby inside. Call a wildlife carer or vet for help. It is sometimes possible to save the baby even though the mother may have passed away."

YOU WILL NEED:

> » A pet carrier lined with a soft towel—a box will not have enough ventilation
> » Extra towels to cover the animal if needed
> » Thick gloves for handling animals that may bite or scratch
> » Bandages or dressings to stop bleeding
> » A bottle of water and a cup for the animal to drink from
> » Contact information for a twenty-four-hour vet and wildlife rescue center

» A dog lead and collar
» Dog treats
» A can of sweet corn to help catch chickens
» A pen and notepad in case you need to note information
» A flashlight and reflective vest can be handy for dawn or dusk
» Pliers and scissors in case animal is trapped in wire that needs to be cut

ANIMAL ACTION

If you have your rescue kit ready, good for you! You are ready in case you find an animal in need. But if you want to take it a step further and care for rescued wildlife, search the internet for wildlife rescue and see if there is a training course you could do. It is illegal in most states to keep wildlife without a permit, so be sure you have the necessary permits if you are taking care of wild animals.

INTRODUCED SPECIES

I believe that kindness and compassion to animals should extend to those whom people refer to as "pests." Many animals are labeled "pests" or "feral," from insects and rodents who take up residence in our homes to rabbits, foxes, and Indian myna birds. Dingos, goats, camels, and even native icons such as kangaroos are killed in their masses as they are viewed as "pests" by farmers.

The thing to remember is that non-native animals were brought here by humans. It is not their fault that they are here, and it is not an excuse for us to be cruel to them. Farmers love to complain about animals such as fruit bats eating their crops or kangaroos grazing in their pastures. But these animals are just trying to survive. Humans have ruined their homes, so of course these animals are going to try and survive on farmland. There are plenty of non-lethal methods farmers can use to protect their crops.

Many people complain about cats killing birds. I know that sometimes introduced animals do cause harm to native animals, but it is not their fault. Trap, neuter, release is a proven method to control populations of introduced species. A lot of us humans who have come to Australia are not native either, and we cause more damage to wildlife with our huge apartment blocks, land clearing, and giant roads than all the introduced animals put together.

1080 FOX BAIT CRUELTY

As a hen rescuer and carer, I consider it my responsibility to ensure the safety of my feathered friends. It is heartbreaking to hear that some of our adoption applicants kill foxes or condone the use of baits. Foxes are just trying to survive. They were introduced into Australia by humans who wanted to hunt them for sport. They didn't ask to be here. Saying that, we must take every precaution to protect our animal friends from predators.

The most common method of killing foxes in Australia is 1080 bait. This bait is banned in all but six countries as it is so dangerous to all animals, including humans. Death by 1080 bait is slow and painful, and it hurts any animal who eats it, not just foxes.

ANIMAL ACTION

If 1080 baiting is taking place in your community, go to Henrescue. org/live-kind/1080-fox-bait and print out double sided copies of our fact sheet. You can also visit PredatorDefense.org for more information on 1080 and other poisons being used in the United States (PredatorDefense.org/docs/wildlife_poisons_fact_sheet.pdf).

Once you have a fact sheet printed, you can then distribute to your local area. It is perfect for a letterbox drop.

If other methods of killing wild animals are happening in your community, you could use this leaflet as inspiration to create your own specific letterbox drop fact sheet.

GO PLASTIC-FREE TO SAVE THE SEAS

You may have seen disturbing photos of seabirds with plastic rings around their necks or turtles with plastic straws stuck in their nostrils. Plastic waste is a massive issue for our oceans and wild areas. In high school, my BFF Melissa and I collected litter from all around the school grounds in an effort to protect the local wildlife. The only problem was the litter didn't fit in the bins, so we stored it in our lockers and forgot about it. Not the smartest idea, and it resulted in a telling-off from the teacher, but we knew we'd made a difference to the local wildlife. It is a fun way to spend time with friends, get outside in beautiful areas, and clean up the environment.

It's not just about collecting litter and recycling but also reducing our consumption of single-use plastic in the first place. Think of all the plastic being manufactured right now. So many bottles and so much packaging that is never going to go away. Even if recycled or disposed of in a bin, it causes massive issues for our planet.

Google "zero waste" to find out how you can reduce your impact on the environment.

Hannah Testa (15) of Atlanta, Georgia, is on a mission to bring an end to single-use plastic. Read the interview below for some serious inspiration, and find out why ridding our oceans and natural environments of litter directly saves animals.

Hannah, how does plastic pollution affect animals?

I watched a documentary called *Plastic Paradise*. It's a film about the Great Pacific Garbage Patch and how it affects wildlife. It changed my life. It was eye-opening. I learnt that around one million seabirds die each year due to plastic pollution. The number keeps growing, as plastic does not biodegrade like most materials. Every single piece of plastic that has ever been made still exists and is still somewhere on our planet, and most of it ends up in our oceans.

Even if you don't live near a lake or a stream, you are still having an impact as plastic goes down into the sewers and ends up in the ocean. It lasts forever, and it gets entangled or ingested by animals. It stays in their stomach and makes them feel like they're full. They often starve or choke to death. I've seen horrible pictures of animals suffering because of our litter.

I have found pieces of plastic that have bite marks where you can see fish or turtles have taken a bite. I show these in a lot of my presentations. Turtles also mistake popped balloons or plastic bags for jellyfish.

Scientists have shown that plastic is in our food chain. Some people eat fish, and fish eat plastic. It's not something happening in the future. It's happening now.

DID YOU KNOW?

The single biggest cause of plastic pollution in our oceans is waste from the fishing industry. So the best way to tackle plastic waste is to stop eating fish and other animals from the ocean.

How can other young people address the issue of plastic pollution in their town?

Start by stopping your use of single-use plastic products such as plastic bags, bottles, straws, and utensils.

If you think about it, it's pretty easy to take reusable bags to stores. Some stores will even give you money back if you bring in your own bag. An average American uses five hundred bags every year. A family of four could use two thousand bags that end up in landfill or streams and oceans every year.

Plastic straws are a big problem. They can't be recycled at all. They are pointless unless you are physically unable to sip from a cup. A lot of people take one mindlessly. There are paper, glass, and stainless steel straws. It is so simple to tell the waiter, "Please, no straw."

Single-use plastic bottles are another big problem. Get yourself a reusable bottle and take it everywhere. I take mine to school with me.

My family have our own mini utensils we use made from bamboo or steel. It's easy to take them around so we can say no to single-use plastic. When collecting litter, I find loads of plastic cutlery.

You've written a book called *Taking on the Plastics Crisis*. Can you tell me a bit about the book?

Taking on the Plastic Crisis is all about the problem with single-use plastics and how to get involved in the fight to reduce plastic pollution. Future activists can read my story, find out how they can get involved with any issue, and hopefully find some inspiration to speak up and stand up.

To take it further ...

Hannah organized a Plastic Pollution Awareness Day in her county, where she screened the documentary *Plastic Paradise* and did a presentation to her community.

Hannah Testa campaigning against single-use plastic

Go to Hannah4Change.org for more information on the amazing work Hannah has done to save the environment.

ANIMAL ACTION

Get together with friends or your animal rights team and head to the beach, river, or anywhere else you've noticed litter. Collect as many straws, bottles, and other litter as you can. Take a pic and share your haul on your socials to inspire others to get active.

Recycle any plastic that is recyclable. You might even make some money by taking bottles to recycle centers. Just think … with every piece of litter you collect, you could be saving the life of an animal, not to mention making their home a whole lot nicer. Wear a vegan message T-shirt at the same time, and you can double down on your activism.

CHAPTER 13

SPEAK UP!

Public speaking is a powerful way to tell people the truth about what is happening to animals. While it can be nerve-racking, it is a way to share stories and help people understand issues and discover ways they can help animals. Many of the young activists in this book have decided to use public speaking to make the world a better place.

INSPIRATION

Haile Thomas (19) of New York City is an experienced public speaker and uses her platform to promote healthy, plant-based eating. She has given two TEDx Talks, and she has also publicly introduced Michelle Obama.

"As someone who uses public speaking as a form of advocacy," says Haile, pictured below, "I would say being authentic yet intentional with your mission and message is very important. I think as young people looking to make a difference in the world, it is so important to prioritize taking care of our mental, physical, and spiritual well-being. Nourishing ourselves is a key part in having the energy to serve our local and global communities."

Charlize Reynierse (22) of Sydney, Australia, uses public speaking as a way to share the stories of animals she has filmed in her undercover work. "Public speaking is not my strong point. I absolutely hate it, and I get so anxious that my voice shakes, which makes me sound like I'm about to cry. I get short of breath, and I struggle with eye contact. But if I can do it, so can you. I think the best way is to speak from the heart. Write something personal, read it to a close friend, and see how they react. When I wrote my speech that I shared at the Animal Rights March, I read it to a couple of friends first, who were all speechless or in tears at the end. That showed me I had portrayed what I wanted to portray. I think when you're speaking about something you're passionate about, the anxiety/nerves become a little less obvious."

Hannah Testa (15) of Atlanta, Georgia, has traveled around the world educating people about plastic pollution. "I'm still a normal person, and I still get nervous before every single speech I do," she says. "Over time, I have learned to handle my nervousness a bit better, so it doesn't look like I'm scared at all."

HANNAH'S PUBLIC SPEAKING TIPS

Have a script. Some people prefer to work from bullet points, but I still have a script, even if I don't use it. It's a comfort thing.

Practice. I spend many hours going through my speech, trying to learn most of it by heart so I don't have to keep looking through my paper.

Make eye contact. Making eye contact is important. Look into the crowd, and look around. When you make eye contact with people, it feels more like having a conversation rather than just standing on a podium and speaking.

"To find speaking opportunities, just send an email to the organization you are interested in speaking at," Hannah says. "Tell them what you want to talk about and why you chose them. Tell them why the topic is so important and how excited you are by the opportunity."

Bailey Mason (16) of Sydney, Australia, uses public speaking as a way to move forward his campaign against keeping dolphins in captivity. Every time I watch him speak, he teaches me something new. He speaks with such passion and knows his subject matter inside out. Bailey also inspired me to forget my own fear of public speaking and think of the animals. Keeping the animals at the forefront of my mind really helped push away the nerves.

"Public speaking is an amazing way to be a voice for the animals," Bailey says. "You can educate people about why you are passionate about animal rights. If you're nervous, that's okay. If you really want to do it, go for it and don't let others discourage you. You have a right to speak up for the animals. You don't have to be perfect. What matters is that you're speaking, and people will listen."

"THE ANIMALS DON'T MIND HOW YOU ARE SPEAKING UP FOR THEM, AS LONG AS YOU ARE SPEAKING UP FOR THEM." — BAILEY MASON

Charlotte Lim (22) of Sydney, Australia, is an experienced public speaker and has presented her own research related to veganism and animal rights at the 6th Conference of the European Association for Critical Animal Studies in Barcelona.

Charlotte says, "Public speaking is one skill that I love using as a form of advocacy. I love talking to people, and being able to convey what I'm passionate about gives me so much energy. The most important thing is to be educated and well informed on your topic so you can answer any tricky questions thrown at you. As a young person, being confident and being strong about your convictions to veganism are absolutely essential when speaking out."

HOW TO PREPARE YOUR SPEECH

» **Choose a topic.** Write all your ideas on a piece of paper. What do you care about? What would you like to tell others? What do you think people need to know?

» **Find somewhere to speak.** It may be as simple as asking your teacher if you can talk in class or in an assembly. Maybe you have an idea for a talk that would be good to present at a vegan festival. Contact your local VegFest and see if they will let you speak. A lot of people would love to hear from more young voices. Just look at Bailey, Charlotte, Hannah, Charlize, and Haile—as well as Vegan Evan, Zoe Rosenberg, and Ateret Goldman—to name just a few young people who regularly speak up for animals.

» **Choose the goals of your talk,** and try to narrow it down to three main points. The aim should be to leave your audience with something new, kind of like a gift. Is there knowledge you can share with them? Do you want to inspire them to take action? Write down your goals. This will help you with your outline.

» **Create a spider diagram** with everything you would like to include in the talk. Stories are a great way to help people relate to your topic. Is there a story about an individual animal that you can tell?

» **Make an outline.** A good speech structure may be an introduction, three main points (each with a different point about your main topic), and a conclusion. The introduction can explain who you are and give a little teaser of what is to come. Each main point should include a story to highlight it. The conclusion should sum everything up and give people a final action or point to take away.

» **Draft your speech or make bullet points.** Some people like to write out their whole speech and then memorize it. Other people (like me) prefer to write bullet points of their main points and then speak from the heart. Try not to read your speech as you will connect better with your audience when making eye contact.

» **Decide if you want to make a PowerPoint presentation.** If you decide to use images, then try not to cram too many words on each slide. You don't want people reading instead of listening to you. Instead, use powerful images that support your words.

» **Practice your speech and check that it fits into the allotted time.**

» **Practice, practice, practice some more.** The more you practice, the less nervous you will be on the day.

» **Keep calm and think of the animals.** Remember Bailey's words: "The animals don't mind how you are speaking up for them, as long as you are speaking up for them."

Don't beat yourself up and try to be perfect. Just the fact that you are trying is enough. Take some index cards with you so if you lose your place you can glance down and remember what you were planning to say next. But if all else fails, just take a deep breath and speak from the heart.

INSPIRATION

Zoe Rosenberg (15), San Luis Obispo, California
"I find that telling stories of individual animals can be so inspiring. I love feeling like I'm inspiring people to take action for animals. That is an amazing feeling. I think providing a message of hope and helping people connect with the animals you have connected with just by speaking about them can be so powerful."

CHAPTER 14

ANIMAL LIBERATION!

As you read this book, you will find certain areas of activism that resonate with you. You may take to protesting like a duck to water, you may start a YouTube channel about veganism that takes off like a fruit bat into the night sky, or perhaps you love letter writing more than a pig loves belly rubs.

The activism that I am most drawn to is animal liberation, the act of freeing animals from the confines of the animal use industries.

While vegan advocacy is so important, there is something special about holding a liberated animal in my arms. As I hold her I promise her that she will be safe and loved. I carry her away from her life of horror into a life of hope. Animal liberation is doing something for the individuals who are stuck in the system right now. When combined with vegan advocacy it becomes incredibly powerful.

SAVING ONE ANIMAL MAY NOT CHANGE THE WORLD, BUT IT WILL CHANGE THE WORLD FOR THAT ONE ANIMAL.

ATERET GOLDMAN'S FIRST RESCUE

We went to a slaughterhouse in San Francisco. We had organized hundreds of activists standing outside, completely non-violent, but with white flowers in their hands. We were bearing witness, being there and taking action. We were able to walk into that slaughterhouse and take animals who were literally about to be killed. We were able to rescue them. I had the privilege of being there and being able to receive this chicken, named Hope, who had only faced violence, torment, machines, and cold hearts for her entire life. I was able to give her her first moment of love. I was able to bring her to a sanctuary where she could feel sunshine for the first time, where she has friends and she's free. So that was an incredible moment.

It was only possible because we had the strength of numbers. We had hundreds of dedicated activists who were there, completely non-violently, but being there for the animals. This was unlike the business, which was there for profit, greed, and tradition—all things we can do away with. It was powerful, and it's only going to get better as our movement grows.

We want to see these rescues happen in every single slaughterhouse and every single farm.

Zoe Rosenberg (15), friend of Ateret and founder of Happy Hen Animal Sanctuary (HappyHen.org), was at the same rescue.

Several activists marched inside a slaughterhouse. Myself and a few other animal caretakers were waiting outside. Outside the slaughterhouse, it was really hard knowing we could only take six hens out. It was hard to see thousands of hens in the slaughterhouse. As the activists came out, I took a hen named Lero. I took her back to the car. Sitting in the car, waiting for the others, I was sad knowing we would have to drive away and leave all those poor chickens behind.

You are safe now little one

Lero was so scared. Her eyes were wide. As they were carrying her out she was screaming, as she expected she would be slaughtered. She had seen some of her sisters being killed, and she thought she would be next. She was terrified.

But she has warmed up to humans so quickly. She loves attention. She and her sisters were really sick upon rescue. We have saved over six hundred chickens, and we've never seen hens as sick as they were. They had the most awful infections. Their eyes were filled with pus. I can't comprehend what they went through to end up in such a state. They would sneeze every two seconds. It was so bad.

As I was walking away, I was speaking to Lero. I said, "Someday there are going to be thousands of activists. There will be hundreds of thousands of us, and we will march inside of every single slaughterhouse and leave with every animal." I promised her that someday soon all animals will be free. That's what got me through it.

Zoe and Lero

A NOTE ABOUT BUYING ANIMALS

Sometimes it feels like the best way to save animals from farms and saleyards is to buy them. Some sanctuaries do buy animals to save them from slaughter, and I understand that. They are desperate to save them, and the animal does not care how they are saved. They just want to live.

But we must keep in mind that by paying for these animals, we are putting money into the pockets of the people who use them. It is a decision each person has to make on their own. But I do not do it for the same reason I do not buy puppies from pet shops.

MY FIRST HEN RESCUE

In 2010 I started NSW Hen Rescue. I was already vegan after finding out the truth about the animal industries, but I felt the burning desire to do more. Veganism seemed like the bare minimum when there was so much suffering in the world. I was aware that in the UK there were various schemes to rehome at least some of the ex-factory-farmed hens (known as *spent hens*) at the end of their use, but here in Australia I didn't know of any such scheme. Once laying hens reach eighteen months of age, their egg production slows slightly, and they can become prone to egg peritonitis and tumors due to their selective breeding. Since the egg industry is all about profit, that means one thing—slaughter. I was interested in rescuing and rehoming some of these girls.

I thought that by adopting some of these "spent hens" I could help to educate people, not only about the state of the hens once they have spent eighteen months in the egg industry, but also about how wonderful chickens are—as friends, not food.

I decided to call my local egg farm and ask a few questions. Considering this farmer had stated in a local paper that he "loves the chickens," it was interesting to see how he was unable to envisage them as anything but profit-making machines.

Me: Hi there, just wondering whether you would be open to rehoming any of the old chickens there?

Farmer: Yeah, we sell chickens. There's a waiting list though, so …

Me: Um, a waiting list? Is that for new chickens coming in?

Farmer: Yeah, they're young birds. Should be delivered end of July.

Me: Sorry, I was inquiring about the older birds. You know, the ones who aren't as productive anymore. Do you rehome any of those?

Farmer: Oh … the old ones. Well, we're getting rid of the old ones in July, but they don't lay so many eggs anymore, so you won't want them.

Me: That's okay, I was just looking for them as companions, so I'm not worried about eggs.

Farmer: You don't seem to understand. These are old hens. They won't lay eggs, and you will still have to feed them. They look really old.

Me: That's fine by me. I don't mind about the eggs. How old are they?

Farmer: They're eighteen months. Some could be a bit older, but they look old, you know?

Me: Yeah, I understand. So how long do chickens live for?

Farmer: Well, they live forever, but you still have to feed them, and you don't get any eggs in return, so there's no point … Anyway, these old birds are going to the land of God.

Me: Right. So would I be able to get some of those birds that are being sent off?

Farmer: Hang on … [He yells off into distance.] Hey … are we going to give away any of the old ones?

Farmer: [To me] No, not now. You would have to phone back mid-July. You should just get the young chickens; that way you can get eggs. I'll put you down for that. Otherwise it's like throwing food into a bin and not getting anything back.

Me: Okay, I'll phone back at the beginning of July, but I am interested in the old chickens. The ones that are being sent to slaughter.

Farmer: Well, maybe you could take a couple, but you will probably regret it when you don't get any eggs. You do realize that you have to feed chickens? Even if they don't lay eggs?

Me: Yes, thank you for your time. I will talk to you in July.

I think we both left that conversation feeling a bit confused. All I know is that after suffering in a cage for eighteen months, these hens deserved to be saved.

The spark of an idea to help these hens was compounded when later that week I attended a local animal rights meeting where we watched a documentary called *Peaceable Kingdom.*

Through the stories of farmers who have experienced an awakening of consciousness, the film portrays the way farmed animals are used and shows what farm sanctuaries are doing to try and help these animals.

One of the most powerful elements of this film was the way that the blissful footage of the animals at Farm Sanctuary sharply contrasted with the horrific treatment of animals at the farms, stockyards, and slaughterhouses. I went from feeling joyful at the compassion shown by the people at the sanctuary to feeling pure rage as I saw a newborn calf being dragged by the leg and beaten.

The end of the film was perhaps the most powerful of all. Horrific images of animal abuse were shown while Moby's haunting song "Why does my heart feel so bad?" was played. Then we were shown hopeful footage of battery chickens who had been rescued being taken into Farm Sanctuary, all in time with the music. Every one of us in the meeting was moved by the film. We were speechless.

I had such a terrible headache after the roller-coaster ride of emotions. But the next day I was feeling less rage and more motivation. I had the Moby song stuck in my head, and I resolved to try to hang on to the feeling of pure outrage because I knew it would help me take action. It is strange how our brains try to push these things to the back of our minds. That day, I began the search for land to rent for the rescued hens.

With this new resolve, I approached the egg farmer again and finally got him to agree to let me and my friend Sharron rescue our first six battery hens.

The day we rescued the girls was my first time in a factory farm. It was overwhelming going to see the hens. So many rows of suffering within this archaic system of farming in which no animal is treated with compassion or as an individual. And this was one of the better farms.

Choosing was hard. I looked around from cage to cage, knowing that every single girl needed help. But one little hen caught my eye. One of her eyes was clouded, and her chest was red raw and bald. Once I made contact with her good eye, that was it. She was the one.

And then I saw her sisters, and Sharron and I made the decision that we needed to save all six girls from the cage. The farmer dragged them out by their feet, and I noticed the blind girl vomited water out of her mouth. I tried to keep my mouth shut as I was trying to secure the release of the hens. As soon as they were in our car, their suffering ended. We placed three girls in each pet carrier. The carriers were padded with soft towels. The hens settled down in the darkness, and off we went to their temporary home.

Sharron and I sat on my balcony and opened the carriers, allowing the girls their first look at their new surroundings. You should have seen their reaction to the sun! I can only imagine how it must have felt to see the brightness and feel that warmth for the first time. They stretched their long necks and basked. Looking around, they didn't seem to believe where they were.

It took quite some time for them to realize that their wings were no longer confined, but when they did, they seemed to relish stretching them out and fanning their feathers. After eighteen months of standing on a wire floor in a cage, this was all new to them. We saw that they had all been debeaked (as all battery hens and most free range hens are). Some still had most of their beak, while others had a long lower beak and short upper beak. Some had obviously been cut too short. A hen's beak is full of nerves, so it is very painful when they have their beaks cut.

We named one of the hens Lizzie, as she kept flicking out her tongue like a lizard, catching bits of dust that showed up in the sun. Before that we hadn't even realized that hens had tongues (yes, we were newbies).

There were many moments during that day when Sharron and I looked at each other, beaming, as we saw how much the hens were enjoying themselves. I remember Sharron sitting with one of the hens on her lap, looking down at her little bald head. We named that girl Britney after the pop star.

It was then time to introduce the girls to their new home. We gently carried them to the coop and placed them on the grass. At first they stood there, unsure what to do next. It was the girl who was blind in one eye who was the most adventurous. She was the first to go tearing off to explore the bushes. We named her Dora the Explorer.

After a while, all the hens began to slowly put one foot in front of the other and walk. They kept looking at their feet as if they were thinking, "I didn't know these things could move like this." It didn't take long before they started to explore and peck and scratch at the ground.

That night, I had to lift each hen up into her roosting area, as they didn't trust the ramp. They loved the cozy straw up there, and, when I peeped in a few minutes later, they were all snuggled in after their busy day.

That night I couldn't sleep, thinking of all the hens stuck in egg farms around the world, unable to express any natural behavior. Sometimes it is overwhelming. But that thought kept me going, and Sharron and I went on to rescue and rehome hundreds more hens from the same farm.

At the end of the rescue, the farmer demanded money from us. He said, "How else can I afford to go on holiday?"

I told him there was no holiday for the hens. It was then that I realized I wasn't content working within the oppressive farming system. I had to challenge the laws that hold these animals as property.

Sharron with rescued friends Britney, Lizzie, and Dora

Every day, there are more and more rescues taking place across the world, and it fills my heart with hope and joy. I truly believe in Ateret's and Zoe's vision that one day we will see rescues happening in every slaughterhouse, farm, and laboratory. We have to; this situation is so urgent, and if we can save one life, then we absolutely should.

CHAPTER 15

UNDERCOVER ACTIVIST

Many forms of animal rights activism rely on the work of undercover investigators. These brave people take footage and photos of what animals experience in animal agriculture and share it with the public. This is the footage that is shown in Cubes of Truth for video activism. It is the footage that has shut down slaughterhouses and won animal cruelty cases. It is the footage that has convinced many people to go vegan. It is the footage that prompted me to start NSW Hen Rescue. It is also the footage that has scared many animal abusers into lobbying governments to introduce ag-gag laws.

AG-GAG LAWS

The work of undercover investigators exposing cruelty may result in a farm being fined, receiving public backlash, or even being shut down. As more farms are exposed for cruelty, other farmers start to get angry and afraid that their farm and cruel practices will be exposed next. In an effort to protect their profit, farmers and agricultural industry advocacy groups lobby politicians for protection.

Some states have introduced ag-gag laws, which ban filming or photography on a farm without the farmer's prior consent. Other forms of ag-gag laws prevent "agricultural fraud," which is when someone applies for a job at a farm with the intention of documenting what is going on at the facility. Starting as state laws in America, ag-gag laws are now in effect in France, Canada, and Australia and are spreading around the world.

In Australia, ag-gag laws insist that if you document animal cruelty, you must turn the evidence in to authorities within twenty-four hours. This prevents activists building a case of ongoing and systemic animal cruelty on a farm and gives the farmer time to cover up any evidence. Australian ag-gag laws also prevent the media from publishing any footage that may have been taken "illegally."

In America, organizations have legally challenged ag-gag laws as unconstitutional, as they violate the First Amendment right of freedom of speech. If a worker wants to speak out against the animal cruelty they are seeing at work, they legally cannot in states that have ag-gag laws. In Utah, Wyoming, Idaho, Iowa, Kansas, and North Carolina, ag-gag laws were found to be unconstitutional and were overturned. Activists and many workers believe that ag-gag laws are an effort to protect profit and business while persecuting those who are trying to expose the cruelty. In effect, these laws protect the abusers and aim to keep animal abuse hidden away where it can't be as easily criticized.

It is important that we challenge these ag-gag laws because animal suffering must be exposed. The idea that workers are not even allowed to share what is going on prevents whistleblowing in the industry.

WHISTLEBLOWERS

A whistleblower is someone who sees something they think may be illegal or unethical and reports it to management or authorities. For example, if I were working as an administrative assistant and saw a culture of racism and bullying in the workplace, I may make notes and take evidence of what I was seeing and report it to upper management so they could deal with the problem. If management refused to take action, I may go to the media in an effort to force change. It is important that all workers feel able to blow the whistle if something immoral or illegal is happening at work to ensure a safe workplace.

Ag-gag laws are an effort to silence whistleblowers on factory farms. That is why you will see that workers' unions are also against ag-gag laws. In Australia, there are laws in place to protect whistleblowers in the workplace, with the exception being whistleblowers within animal agriculture.

FIGHTING AG-GAG LAWS

Ag-gag laws are another hurdle that big ag and the government have put in place to try and stop us standing up for animals. It's important to fight these laws at a legislative level. Contact your local MP or senator. Check out our letter-writing page for inspiration, and get writing! Letters, emails, and petitions can make a difference. If you want to do more, contact the Animal Legal Defense Fund, which challenges ag-gag laws in America. Visit ALDF.org for more information and to sign the petition.

Types of Undercover Investigations

Covert investigation

Perhaps the most well-known form of undercover investigation is when an activist enters a property without the knowledge of the owner. They will take photographs or videos of what they see. These photos and images may be shared on social media or given to the mainstream media at a later date.

Camera installs

A camera install may take place as part of a covert or workplace investigation. The activist will place hidden cameras around the facility in areas where work with animals takes place. After a time, the investigator will watch the footage to see what has been captured. Camera installs may also be used in domestic cruelty cases. For example, in Australia a dog is not legally allowed to be chained twenty-four hours a day, but it is very easy for someone to say, "Oh, but I do let my dog off the chain for an hour every day, just when you are not here." An animal cruelty officer may set up a camera to show that in fact the dog is not ever let off the chain over a twenty-four-hour period. That evidence would allow the authorities to take action to help the dog.

Interviews

A legal form of investigation is to interview people who work at the agriculture facility. In her book *Slaughterhouse*, Gail Eisnitz spoke to many slaughterhouse workers and was able to gather a complete picture of the workplace. Despite not including photos or videos, the interviews were harrowing to read and conveyed just what horror the animals and the workers go through in slaughterhouses.

Investigation at work

This is a form of undercover investigation used a lot by organizations like Mercy for Animals. It is one kind of investigation that some states have ag-gag laws to try and outlaw. An activist will apply for a job at an animal use facility like a factory farm, dairy, or slaughterhouse. The person will do the job for however long it takes to gather enough evidence to show what happens there. They will wear a button camera or other device to document what they have to do at work and what they see others do.

Not everyone who exposes workplaces for cruel practices is an activist. Some workers on live export ships, at slaughterhouses, and at factory farms are so appalled by the working conditions and what is done to animals that they will document what they are experiencing and later contact the media. This is an example of whistleblowing that ag-gag laws try to prevent.

Legal investigation when visiting a place of animal use

As a member of the public, it is legal to attend many places of animal use. For example, in Australia anyone can attend a saleyard where animals are auctioned off to various slaughterhouses. It is legal to take photos or videos while visiting these places, although it may be frowned upon. The same would be true if you were visiting a public pet shop that had horrible conditions. You could take photos or video and take it to the authorities. While this does not have to be done undercover, it is the preferred method as the saleyard workers or pet shop staff would certainly frown upon footage being taken.

Occasionally a slaughterhouse or farm may allow a journalist to come onto the property and take photos and videos with permission. Due to the nature of what happens in these places, even these photos and videos can often be harrowing.

Investigation at a vigil or protest

Many activists choose to take photos or videos when they attend vigils or protests at places of animal use. They may film the animals who are in the truck about to go into the slaughterhouse. This is legal and can show the conditions the animals arrive in. It can be useful to share with friends and family and to help share the stories of individual animals.

Drone investigation

A method of investigation that was used a lot in the animal rights documentary *Dominion* was drone footage. Different parts of the world have different laws on using drones, but in some areas it is legal to fly a drone over a farm to get a view from above. This can yield high-quality footage and help to show the sheer scale of factory farm operations. It is a way to gather evidence from large properties. For example, if cattle have no shade in a boiling hot feedlot, drone footage could allow someone to film how many cattle have no shade and whether any of the animals have died.

THE *DOMINION* MOVEMENT AND ANNIVERSARY ACTIONS

In March 2018, a feature-length Australian documentary was released that uses evidence from undercover investigators as well as drone footage to expose the truth about the Australian agricultural industry.

The film has been screened around the world and has resulted in a huge number of new vegans. So many different farms and different forms of animal use were included that it was impossible for people to write the harrowing footage off as "just one bad farm." Like *Earthlings* before it, *Dominion* is an example of what can be done with undercover footage and how it can bring about change for animals.

In April 2019, a number of actions were held around Australia to mark the one-year anniversary of the film. This included slaughterhouse shutdowns and protestors blocking the busiest intersection in Melbourne. The actions got a huge amount of attention and resulted in thousands more people viewing the documentary. One activist who was involved in the *Dominion* film and the *Dominion* anniversary actions was Charlize Reynierse.

ACTIVIST PROFILE

Charlize Reynierse (22), Sydney, Australia

Charlize has already built up an impressive catalog of photos and videos from her undercover activism. She has helped to expose slaughterhouses and factory farms, and she provided a large amount of footage that was used in *Dominion* and is currently used in video activism in Sydney and around the world.

What excites you most about your activism?

I can leave the world a better place than when I first entered it. Being vegan is good, but that just means you stop contributing to the problem, rather than taking steps to fix the problem. Activism helps me know I have done something in my life to make a difference. It excites me seeing how many more people are going vegan and how much more mainstream it is becoming.

How did you get involved in undercover investigation?

I started with legal investigation work. I would go to saleyards in the day and document what I saw. I would take photos of the animals waiting to be sold and the conditions that they were kept in. I started a photography page on Facebook to anonymously share what I had found and to tell the stories of these animals. When I saw how effective sharing their stories was, I wanted to expand on my investigations.

I started doing undercover investigations, which allowed me to document how these animals lived and what they went through. As well as taking videos and photos of the animals I met, I also installed hidden cameras to document what happened in the day.

I have done undercover work where I work legally in a facility but take the opportunity to take footage whilst I am there. This has seen me working in places like piggeries, hatcheries, meat farms, and slaughterhouses.

I feel that workplace undercover activism is the most effective. I have found I can get very unique footage that would otherwise be impossible to get. It seems to be more widely shared than other footage. Maybe because it is from the perspective of a worker, people know that it is a truthful representation.

Can you tell me why undercover investigation is so important to the animal rights movement?

I think that almost all other forms of activism rely on the work of undercover activists. For example, video activism like The Cube of Truth could not exist without undercover investigations. I would say most people go vegan for ethical reasons, and they often do this because they saw awful footage of what happens to animals.

I think it is essential that we keep doing undercover work so that we always have up-to-date footage and no one can say, "Things are different now. That was from ten years ago." I also think the more undercover footage we get, even if it is of the same thing, the more it shows how much of a systemic issue cruelty in animal agriculture is. It eliminates the argument of, "Oh, not all chicken farmers are like that." How could anyone say that if there is footage from twenty different chicken farms showing the same thing?

I run an anonymous photography page on Facebook where I tell the stories of individual animals to try to get people to make an emotional connection to individuals. So often in investigations, we have footage of thousands of animals, and there is no focus on specific individuals. The scale of it all is overwhelming, so I think focusing on telling the stories of individuals is extremely important. Social media is probably one of the most effective ways of spreading veganism, so building a social media platform without having to put my name to it really appealed to me.

You are an animal rights photographer. Can you talk a bit about the power of photography to tell the stories of animals?

Through photography, we can capture the essence of individual animals. The specific look in their eyes. The way they look at humans, the way they look at their own kind. The way they huddle together in the dark. I think so many people connect to the message behind veganism visually in some way. Really good quality photos are essential for big banners and signs like those used in the *Dominion* anniversary actions. I think that when the world finally goes vegan, these photos are going to be in history books. I feel like if I take photos, then the animals won't go unseen. Someone saw them. I, at the very least, saw them amongst the thousands of lives. They weren't just another number, another statistic.

If a young person wants to use photography or film to help animals, what advice would you give them?

Don't worry too much about the quality of your camera; just start with what you have. Watch YouTube videos on photography and practice at home. Try to go to places you are legally allowed to be, like saleyards and vigils, to practice your animal photography. It's really hard to take photos of stressed-out moving animals, even in the daytime, and even more so at night. Take your camera with you everywhere. If you're driving and you see a paddock full of dairy calves, pull over and see if you can get any good photos without trespassing. At saleyards, I generally find that asking the manager if it's okay to take photos for a uni project works well; they usually say yes.

You have had to leave many animals behind in your activism, but you have also had the opportunity to save lives. Can you tell me about why rescue is important to you?

Every single individual matters. Even rescuing one life means the world for that one individual. Rescue is so rewarding, especially in investigations. You usually have to wait until the end of the investigation, so you have seen these animals suffering for so long, and to finally get to rescue even just a tiny number is so rewarding. Rescue is also important because while people need to see what happens to animals in farms, they also need to see what these animals are like when they are in a happy, safe, healthy environment. The contrast between the animals in the farm and the animals once they're rescued makes it so obvious that animals just want to be free.

What kind of personality/character traits do you think someone needs to do undercover work?

Different kinds of work require different kinds of people. For investigative work where we visit farms covertly to take footage or install cameras, we need people who are dedicated, patient, and strong-willed. It's definitely not something that's suited to everyone, and it can be really exhausting, emotional, thankless work. It can be physically exhausting. There can be hours of waiting, but in the end, it's all worth it. Being able to work in a team is also essential.

Can you tell me about some of your experiences working undercover?

This form of activism hasn't always appealed to me; I sort of just fell into it. No one had told me how to go about it or anything. I was just in a specific circumstance where I had to work on a farm, so I chose a really big one, took a camera, earnt a lot of trust, and got a lot of really damning footage. For me, it was quite opportunistic.

The first placement I did was the piggery. It lasted for three weeks. The facility was so isolated, and I dreaded having to be away from loved ones for such an extended amount of time in a place I knew would affect me deeply. Because I was a student, my assumption was that they would at least try and hide the worst sides of the industry from me. I was wrong. It seemed that things only got worse the longer I was there. The longer I was there, the more people trusted me and the more I witnessed.

I have had some close calls with having my cover blown. You have to think about things like what to eat around people you're working with, what you would do if they offered you animal products, what you would do or say if they asked you to perform certain acts to animals. I have worked undercover in two farms, a hatchery, and two slaughterhouses. All of them were absolutely horrendous. I felt like I had to do it, and once I had done it once and I had shut down a part of myself emotionally, I was somewhat immune to the emotional effects of seeing what happens to animals firsthand, so I felt like I was in the perfect position to continue doing undercover work.

You have been arrested as part of your work for animal rights. Can you talk a bit about these experiences?

I have been arrested three times during my work for animal rights. The first time was the Lakesland case where NSW Hen Rescue had received anonymous footage of a disgusting free range egg farm where hens were being starved and dehydrated to death. The authorities were not taking any action, so we attempted rescue ourselves. We were hoping the police would come and help us with the rescue, but instead they came to arrest us. From this arrest, I learnt that a small group of people can really pull together and make things happen. Sometimes you have to drop everything and do what you can to help animals, and this was one of those cases. So many different people pulled together and used their skills to help the hens.

The second arrest was at the *Dominion* anniversary action, where I took part in a slaughterhouse shutdown where we chained ourselves to the equipment, effectively preventing the slaughter of more animals. From this action, I learnt that you need to do thorough research and make sure you have a trustworthy, cooperative team.

My third arrest was accidental. I was caught on a turkey farm retrieving an installed camera. From this I learnt to *never* be complacent. You really can never get comfortable doing investigative work. Anything can happen at any moment; you always need to be vigilant in terms of checking for cameras, taking your time to listen out for movement, etc.

I believe challenging laws is essential. The Lakesland case is a perfect example of that as we are appealing our guilty conviction. If the appeal is successful, we will have a landmark case where it is recognized that sometimes it is essential to trespass to help animals in dire needs.

We talk about burnout in Chapter 17, but I feel it is especially relevant for undercover activists. What do you do to look after yourself?

Self-care is so important, and something that should not be taken for granted. You should work on self-care during activism well before you experience burnout. I have experienced various mental health issues and burnout, and it really has affected me. I found it really hard because I felt an obligation to keep going even though I was burnt out because if I stopped, less animals would be helped. But it got to a point where I became so much less effective: I was tired, I couldn't even focus, I was irritable. It wasn't good. And it went for a long time; it took me a long time to have the motivation that I had before burnout.

So many activists mistake self-care as a break from activism, when really it is a central part of it.

By practicing self-care, you're ensuring you can help animals for a long time, and you will prevent long periods of burnout where you are completely ineffective. Work out how much you can deal with and do not exceed that. Do not get sucked in to neglecting your basic needs in order to help animals. Have some part of your life that is separate from activism. For me, it's dancing. It has absolutely nothing to do with activism. In terms of dealing with post-traumatic stress disorder (PSTD), this is very complex, and I highly recommend seeking help from a psychiatrist. Try and find someone who specializes in the area, and stick with the therapy.

Where do you see your personal activism taking you in the next ten years?

I hope my activism will continue to ramp up. I definitely see myself being arrested many more times in the next ten years. I hope in the next ten years I will have my own property to have space to care for more rescue animals. I hope I will have written a book in ten years about my experiences, too.

REMEMBERING THEM

Undercover investigators are often in the very difficult position of having to witness and document an animal suffering without being able to help that individual. They need to keep their eyes on the big picture and the fact that the footage they get will help spare many more animals in the future. Despite this, the stories of individuals stick with investigators. On the following pages, Charlize tells us about two individuals she will always remember.

Milo the goat

The goats at the slaughterhouse were particularly fearful. Except for this one. He must not have been a wild goat but perhaps someone's pet, or perhaps a small hobby farm sent him here to his death. I won his trust, giving him lots of head scratches. I called him Milo. Each time I walked away, he would stand up against the fence and paw at it with one of his front legs, beckoning me to come back and return to scratching his adorable little face. I kept coming back, giggling as he leant into the scratches and gave me little goat kisses all over my hands.

Then, I helped with moving the pigs into the gas chamber. Not because I had to but because doing so placed me in a position where I could both film them in the gas chamber and make the production line slightly more efficient, lessening the need for electric prodding the pigs to make them go into the gas chamber.

Just before I went to lunch, I went to pat my goat friend again, but he was terrified of me. I tried not to let this crack me wide open. He could smell the blood from the pigs, and he wanted nothing to do with me. I had betrayed his trust.

I can't get his face out of my head. Each time I think of him, two images flash before my eyes. The way he gazed longingly at me as he stood against the fence, begging me to come back and give him more scratches, and the dull, lifeless look in his eyes after slaughter. I won't forget the way I betrayed his trust.

Stig the pig

She was in a sow stall, and she had just been artificially inseminated for the first time. Scrawled across her back in bright pink spray paint was the word *stig*.

"What does that mean?" I asked.

The worker explained to me that a pig with *stig* spray-painted on them were those who had ripped out the ear tags of other pigs. The word *stig*, at least on this particular farm, referred to any of the three or four different ear tags the sows all had pierced through their ears.

As the worker explained, the pig looked up at me, a silly sort of innocent look etched into her facial features. She stood amongst hundreds of other sows, and she stood out to me as she had adorable and distinctive darker patches on her face and her body. She had a funny box-shaped head, and she refused to let her snout remain dirty. She was forced to dirty it in the first place due to the general filth which surrounded her, out of her own control. But she was regularly seen pressing her nose against the water sprayer, not doing so with the intention of drinking water but cleverly doing so just to clean her nose.

She also had a big circle spray-painted on her back.

I already knew what this meant—that she had failed to conceive the first time she was inseminated, as well as the second time.

"She signed her own death sentence, twice," the worker joked, laughing, proud of his remark.

What he meant was that pigs who are labeled as "stigs" are sent to slaughter as they present an inconvenience in group housing where they chew off other pigs' ear tags, making them unidentifiable. That was her first death sentence.

Her second death sentence was her two failed pregnancies. Two strikes, and she's out. Get pregnant, or die. Perhaps her body was so exhausted from her previous litters that she could no longer go on.

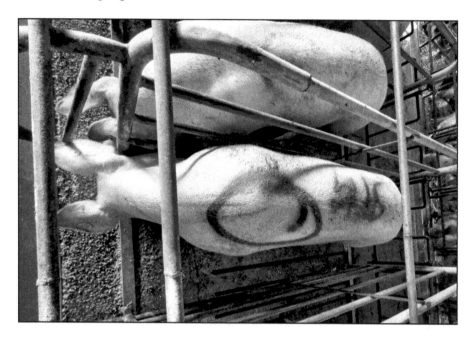

I stared down at her as she made her charismatic little oinks at me. She made me smile in this terrifying, sorrow-filled hell I was in. A hell that was nothing compared to the hell the animals faced. I visited her multiple times a day whilst I worked in the shed she was held captive in. I was met with loving snorts and grunts as I gave her a firm neck rub. As I scratched her neck, making my way towards the back of her ears, she would press herself into my hand, but she would always be careful not to crush my hand against the bars which confined her.

I saw her for who she was.

I knew what was coming for her.

And I knew there was absolutely nothing I could do to stop it.

While these stories are upsetting, sometimes undercover investigations do result in individual animals being helped. In the Lakesland case that Charlize mentioned, an undercover investigator exposed horrible neglect at an egg farm. The authorities were doing nothing to help the hens, but thanks to the footage, NSW Hen Rescue stepped in and was able to save some of the hens, including beautiful Kim.

Kim, happy and healthy at NSW Hen Rescue HQ

Kim is a cheeky hen. If I can't find her at the sanctuary, it is most likely she has hopped into the feed bin to grab some extra snacks. She loves to preen people and always has to know what is going on. She has an implant so she never has to lay eggs again, and she just loves to dust-bathe with her friends. Sometimes I sit on the grass, and Kim and the other girls preen me. I think for a moment of the horrible things Kim has experienced, and then I think of the life she has now. It keeps me going.

Check out these amazing animal rights photographers ...

Tamara Kenneally Photography (TamaraKenneallyPhotography.com)

We Animals Media (WeAnimalsMedia.org)

Animals Within (Facebook.com/animalswithinphotography/)

CHAPTER 16

SANCTUARY LIFE

Something that goes hand-in-hand with animal liberation is sanctuary. A sanctuary is a place where animals are safe, cared for, and loved for life. It is a place where they will never be used or exploited.

At NSW Hen Rescue, we do not have a large property due to lack of funds, so we call our rented house and garden a *vegan microsanctuary*. The special-needs animals we have here are safe for life. They will never be used again.

The point of a farm sanctuary is not to rescue every farmed animal. As much as we want to, there is no way anyone could save all of the billions that are suffering. But each and every life saved is worth the effort, care, and love. At least a few farmed animals will have the chance to express their natural behavior and live a life free from use. Those individuals saved are important. We may not be able to save everyone, but we should save as many individuals as we can.

As well as saving these individuals, another important role of sanctuaries is education. Farm sanctuaries that are open to the public give people a chance to get up close and personal with rescued farmed animals, probably for the first time in their lives. They are also able to share the animals' stories via social media. Watching videos from sanctuaries such as Little Oak Sanctuary or Edgar's Mission, you can see the personalities of these animals. It helps people realize that all animals are individuals. These experiences can be enough for some people to begin questioning the way they live and the choices they make.

Some sanctuaries have education centers where visitors can learn more about the animals they meet and the inhumane way they are used and treated on farms. Even if a small percentage of these people decide to make the change and become vegan, then it is worth it. Some farm sanctuaries offer opportunities for schools to spend the day among the animals. Imagine the impact that day could have on your classmates. Certainly better than a cruel ag program or hatching project.

Even if a sanctuary cannot have open days, it is still able to share the stories of the rescued animals and reach many people via social media or press releases. For example, my friend Melinda the chicken, pictured below, was rescued just down the road from a slaughterhouse. Melinda had a very lucky escape. She had a broken leg and had to have surgery to fix her bones. Despite having a metal contraption on her leg, she zoomed around the house getting into mischief. She was curious and fun-loving. I was able to share the story of Melinda with others to get them thinking about how all chickens in the meat industry have their own personalities and how they all deserve to live free from use.

When I was sixteen, I volunteered at my local animal sanctuary, and it was one of the happiest times of my life. It was where I met my very first vegan activists and where I got to hang out with chickens, ducks, geese, rabbits, and more. But I never thought I could open an animal sanctuary so young.

Charlotte, Zoe, and Wilma

Zoe Rosenberg (15) of San Luis Obispo, California, started Happy Hen Animal Sanctuary when she was only eleven years old.

My mom and I found six chickens who had been abandoned by the side of the road. They were covered in mites. We took them home and we took care of them. That is the moment I realized there are abandoned chickens that need rescuing. I wasn't yet thinking about chickens from the food industry.

I asked my mom, "Hey, can we start a chicken rescue?" and she said, "Maybe." I was like, "Well, it's not a no."

I started a website and created a Facebook page, and when Mom saw that she said, "Okay, we can rescue twelve chickens, but that's it." That's when I emailed NSW Hen Rescue and asked how I could get chickens out of the industry. I got some tips about how to approach farmers and steps to take. We saved hens from a local egg farm. We still have a lot of those girls living with us. Once we saw how much the hens were enjoying their freedom, it didn't feel right to stop there, so we rescued more. We do tours occasionally. Our last tour was for an animal rights club from UC Santa Barbara.

The animals don't love the tours, so we don't do them too often. If people ask if they can pick up a chicken, I tell them they don't like that. I give them a handful of chicken feed, and the chickens can come to them.

Ferdinand is a little silkie rooster we have rescued. He had been abandoned outside of an apartment complex, and his people had moved away. He was just waiting for them to come back, and they never did. The people in the neighboring apartment took pictures of him and were making fun of him on Facebook. They wrote, "Ha-ha, he's still waiting." They were ignoring the fact he was in mourning and upset.

Luckily, a lady who knew the people posting got in touch with a friend in LA, and that friend saved him and brought him to our sanctuary. He has settled in well, and he's quite a sweetie. We get contacted every day about roosters. We are so full with roosters. People need to stop buying and breeding chicks and realize that animals are not disposable.

It's very hard trying to find time for everything. I do school from home, so I have more time for animal care. I generally get up at 5 a.m. so I have more time in the day. I get a lot of schoolwork done before the animals are even awake.

At 7:30 a.m. I go around and let everyone out of their nighttime enclosures. We have several different areas, so it takes about thirty minutes to get everyone out. I feed them and give them water. I do a little cleaning. Then we have a few part-time volunteers who come and help with the animals. At about 5 p.m. I make sure everyone is safely in bed so they are safe from predators.

Caylin King (17) of Newcastle, Australia, runs a private animal sanctuary from home with her mum.

We have 5.5 acres, and we do bird rescue and farmed animal rescue. We recently took in another pig. She is still fairly young. Her name is Freya, and she was advertised needing a home on a Newcastle vegan community site. The people who cared for her lived in suburbia. The couple had broken up and they couldn't keep Freya, so they were looking for a home for her. We already had a pig named Lenore and were looking for another companion for her. We found out that Freya's carers had a nose ring on her to stop her digging, which was terrible. She had scarring inside her nose. She was terrified. Lenore showed her the ropes. She loves digging now.

Caylin hanging out with her rescued animal friends

IS SANCTUARY LIFE FOR YOU?

Running a sanctuary is a huge job. It is not a nine-to-five occupation but something that takes up every aspect of your life. There is so much to think about when starting a sanctuary, and for most young people it is only an option if your parents can support the vet bills and help you with transport.

But sanctuary life is also incredibly rewarding. You get to know animals as good friends and spend time with them happy and content. You get to give back to animals who have been so abused by humans, and watch as they slowly gain confidence. It is important to be realistic with your sanctuary goals. You may be like me and only be able to care for smaller animals like chickens (well, there was the time I fostered six piglets). Maybe it is something you can plan to do when you're older, but the more experience you can get beforehand, the better. It is so sad when we hear of sanctuaries having to rehome animals because they don't have enough funds or have not prepared properly.

THE MICROSANCTUARY MOVEMENT

The microsanctuary movement is based around the idea that any vegan home can be a sanctuary for a liberated animal. Even if you care for one rescued animal, you are still providing that animal with sanctuary. The movement recognizes that it is important that animals are saved from animal agriculture *now*. It promotes the idea that individuals matter, that every life saved is worthwhile and deserves the best of care. It recognizes that while not everyone has a huge property, we can all make a difference.

To find out more about microsanctuaries go to: Microsanctuary.org.

Charlize Reynierse (22), of Sydney, Australia, runs one of the NSW Hen Rescue microsanctuaries from her rented garden.

I adopted four ex-battery hens from NSW Hen Rescue. They were named Zara, Eva, Flop, and Acorn. I remember letting the girls out when I got home from adopting them. They immediately lay down to sunbake. They had never been able to do this before, but it was like an uncontrollable urge they had. As I got to know the girls, I bonded with them and knew I had to do more to help hens like them who were still stuck in the egg industry.

Some time later I had the opportunity to attend a rescue training day at NSW Hen Rescue HQ. On my first rescue I was so excited. I wasn't really nervous. I just wanted to be involved in liberation.

I wanted to care for hens with special needs. I feel that if you can help special-needs animals, you should do it because those animals are the ones not everyone can look after. They are the ones who suffer the most in these farms.

I had been volunteering for NSW Hen Rescue for a while. I was helping with rescues and had filmed and edited some videos and photos. When Catherine asked me if I'd like to run the third microsanctuary, it felt like the natural next step.

We rescued Ahna, Merida, and Mumble from a free-range farm.

Ahna has a lot of nicknames. She is Ahna Banana, Bahn, and Ben. I think she is hilarious because of the sound she makes. We have a word for each of the girls' different noises. Ahna's noise is *meep*, like the road runner. You just hear this high-pitched *meep* every now and again. Ahna has been through a lot. She has had the most vet appointments out of everyone. She weighed only one kilogram when we found her. I didn't even think she'd make it through the night. She had such a bad nasal infection, her face was all swollen. She had to gain weight before it was safe for her to go under anesthetic. The infection just kept coming back. But she recently got an implant to save her from laying eggs, and that seemed to help a lot. She is the healthiest she has ever been. We always say Ahna is the best at scratching. We have what are called "scratch parties," where we throw scratch mix in the long grass. That is pretty much how we mow the lawn at our place. Ahna has the best scratching legs. She kicks grass meters behind her.

DID YOU KNOW?

At NSW Hen Rescue, nearly all our permanent special needs flock have hormonal implants to stop them from laying eggs. The hens we rescue have been selectively bred to lay way too many eggs, and it really takes its toll on their bodies, often leading to reproductive cancer. An implant is the greatest gift we can give the girls. No more eggs and a much longer and happier life.

The same night we saved Ahna, we also saved Merida and Mumble. Merida has the same respiratory issues as Ahna. After a lot of care she beat the infection. Merida has constantly got something to say, and she has this strange obsession with pet carriers. If there is a carrier with a door open she will get in there and have fun. She also loves to jump on anything she can. She is definitely the mischievous one. If something funny has happened in the backyard, you know it was Merida. Like, if someone has eaten my tomato plant, I know immediately it was Merida.

As for Mumble, she has a spinal deformity which means she walks vertically, like a penguin. Mumble is top of the pecking order. But she is a really good queen. We call her Queen Bee or Mumble Bee. Everyone knows that she is on top, but she also looks after everyone. Clementine is at the bottom of the pecking order, as she is newest. She was rescued from a battery cage with very brittle bones and calcium deficiency, which led to her breaking her femur. She needed to have surgery and then was crate-rested for six weeks. Now she has one leg shorter than the other due to the way her leg has healed. The other day Clementine was dust bathing and Mumble was just standing there watching her and guarding her. I have seen her do that with others as well. Mumble is the smartest chicken I have ever met. She has such a long attention span. If she hears me in the kitchen she knows because of where the sound is coming from, and she will come up the stairs and look at me from the window. She knows if she stays there long enough I will come and give her a treat. She is very persistent and will stay there for an hour without getting impatient.

After some time, I took in Eleanor and Wilma. They were from a caged farm. Eleanor had a fused hip joint so she doesn't have much hip mobility. Her leg sticks out at an awkward angle. She sleeps inside as she can't get into the coop. Eleanor is very much a woman of routine. She is probably the most like an elderly lady out of everyone. She likes her routine and she gets very upset if guests come over too often. She sleeps inside and she doesn't like if I have to bring her in early. She is the most well-groomed out of everyone. She loves to preen and has the fluffiest bum in all of NSW Hen Rescue!

Wilma had a neurological issue. When I found her in the cage, her head was tucked underneath her body. She looked stuck. A week later her symptoms had disappeared. I now think she had minor brain damage because she still does some funny things like obsessive pecking sometimes. Wilma is just really sweet and quirky and just a bit special. There is something about her that is a little bit ditzy. She's always on the move. She's always got somewhere she needs to be.

Finally I have Peanut, our little amputee. She was dumped on someone's front doorstep in a box. She had a very deformed leg and needed an amputation. Peanut does not think she is a chicken; she thinks she is a cat. She purrs; she just wants to sit on the couch. She doesn't want to be outside. She is also very smart. When she watches TV, she really watches it and she reacts. Like if there are certain scary scenes she will stretch her neck out. She is very trusting, very dependent, and like my actual child. She wins over everyone who comes to visit.

I always joke to my partner, Aidon, that the hens always come to me normal in their personality and then within a week or two they develop these little quirks. They do such hilarious things. I think chickens are the sweetest animals.

VOLUNTEERING

A great way to gain experience, help animals, and find out if sanctuary life is for you is to volunteer.

One of the best things I have ever done was my volunteer work at an animal sanctuary in the UK while growing up. I had always loved animals and was a vegetarian at the time, but it was the time spent at the sanctuary that made it clear to me that I wanted to dedicate my life to helping animals.

For anyone who is considering making animal rescue a big part of their life, it is a great idea to spend some time volunteering. Not only can you help a charity and gain valuable hands-on experience with animals, but you can also get an idea about whether the sanctuary lifestyle is really for you. Volunteering can be a real eye-opener. It shows you the good (such as when an animal is placed in a wonderful home, or when you are able to offer refuge to stray animals) and the bad (such as when animals fall ill or die). You can also see the huge costs involved in providing food, care, shelter, and veterinary treatment, as well as the massive workload.

As you can see from this photo of **Vegan Evan (7) of Florida** on the next page, volunteering is hands-on and a lot of work—but very rewarding!

The sanctuary I volunteered at was fairly small, but it was a refuge to many animals. There were cats, dogs, rabbits, rats, chinchillas, geese, chickens, ducks, two white donkeys named Ivy and Noel, and a naughty Shetland pony named Dennis. There was also a beautiful Jersey cow named Annabel. There were only ever a few dogs at a time, but the dogs who came in were all placed in wonderful new homes.

I usually helped out (along with my BFF Melissa) in the morning, and our first job was to clean out around fifty cat litter trays (some cats shared). That was a smelly way to start the day, but once all the animals were clean, fed, and watered it felt wonderful, and we would start on the huge pile of washing up.

After all the daily chores, we would enjoy walking the dogs or making play areas for the chinchillas or rabbits.

I have also volunteered at a wildlife sanctuary and a horse sanctuary, and I have helped out with admin work at the offices of various animal rights organizations.

If you would like to volunteer for an animal sanctuary or animal rights organization, do a Google search for your local groups. For example, if you live in Sydney, you could search for *Sydney animal sanctuary*. Then take a look through the results and see whether any websites come up that offer volunteer opportunities. Even if you only have one day free a week, you could make a difference to a charity and gain experience. Running the hen rescue, I really appreciate just how important volunteers are. And being a volunteer myself, I understand how rewarding it can be, too.

Priscilla Huynh (20) of Sydney, Australia, is our regular animal care volunteer here at NSW Hen Rescue.

> I was halfway through studying to be a dietitian when I realized that I wouldn't like to work in that field for longer than five years. With encouragement, I decided to follow my heart and study to be a vet nurse. It was a scary decision, but I now know I made the right one. My dream is to be able to

travel to countries such as Vietnam and Bali and use my skills to volunteer to help animals.

As a requirement of my vet nursing course, I need to complete placement hours working with animals to gain experience and knowledge of animal care. I knew about NSW Hen Rescue through the vegan community online and have always wanted to volunteer. I knew this would be a fantastic opportunity to volunteer at an animal sanctuary whilst gaining the experience and knowledge to pursue my dream.

Volunteering for NSW Hen Rescue is the highlight of my week. Even though it is hard work, it is so therapeutic to be with the animals. They will follow me around the garden as I'm doing my duties. This involves a lot of cleaning of coops, litter trays, carriers, and enclosures. I also feed the animals and assist in health checks and administering medication. Sometimes a hen will get a messy bottom from a reproductive problem. This happens as a result of the egg industry's selective breeding. To help the hen feel comfortable until her vet appointment, we give her a nice warm bath.

Gretel, one of the hens at NSW Hen Rescue HQ, who was liberated from an egg farm, laid two eggs a day. Consequently, she was calcium deficient and had broken her wing in two places. When I first met her, she was timid and didn't like being close to me, which is understandable. After receiving vet treatment and lots of love, she settled in extremely well, and her feathers grew back. When I visited again, I almost didn't recognize her as she was looking so much healthier. Gretel is now a lot more confident around me and will come up to me when I am in the garden. She is so gentle and gets along with the other hens because she doesn't like to cause a fuss. If other hens bicker, Gretel will intervene to try and stop the drama.

ACTIVIST PROFILE

Charlotte Lim (22), Sydney, Australia

What excites you most about activism?

The impact that my actions have on individual animals. Seeing before and after photos of rescued animals and seeing the difference my work has made is what keeps me going. I love being able to help a grassroots organization like NSW Hen Rescue make a real difference to the hens. Spreading the message of veganism is so important since it's my way of helping the world become a better place for both animals and humans.

Bluebelle, pictured before and after, is a hen rescued by NSW Hen Rescue

How did you first become involved in activism?

I started very small. Before I went vegan, I held a birthday party, and instead of having people bring presents, I asked people to donate to a vegan charity, NSW Hen Rescue. I got a bit creative and made a "Wishing Well" box where people could donate cash on the day. Or they could donate online directly. I found that to be a great start to raise awareness of the organization and show my love for animals.

I got more involved in animal activism while at uni and particularly on exchange. I attended an Official Animal Rights March in Copenhagen with over 600 other vegans, which was a phenomenal experience of solidarity. I got to chat to people who were watching the march about veganism and animal rights. I also continued activism via a more academic route when I produced some research and presented my findings at the 6th Conference of the European Association for Critical Animal Studies, held in Barcelona in May of 2019. And now I volunteer at NSW Hen Rescue, so I'm doing activism all the time. From creating and sharing social media content to website building and coop cleaning.

What kind of activism resonates with you most?

I feel that education is a very effective form of activism. I am so thankful for the number of inspirational vegan lecturers and activists I've learned from at university who exposed me to animal rights issues and demonstrated how perfectly being vegan aligned with my other values.

As I've become more involved in the vegan community, I've found "artivism" to be really effective for me. I love seeing what kind of vegan messages can be promoted in a fun and creative way. I really enjoyed doing an animal rights march, but those can be quite physically demanding, and it also depends a lot on the crowd and the people you meet. I have so much respect for the activists who do video activism and expose the cruelty of factory farming to the public and the activists who directly liberate animals and share their stories on social media pages that I follow.

What led you to volunteering, and can you tell us a bit about your experience?

It was my sister who pushed me into volunteering. I didn't have any admin experience and wasn't sure how much use or how good I would be at helping out the organization. I just wanted to help animals, and having grown up surrounded by birds like chickens, quails, pigeons, and cockatiels, NSW Hen Rescue seemed like the perfect organization to volunteer for. I'm so glad I took that leap of faith and volunteered; my experience has been so wonderful. I get to help animals each and every day, I get to spend time with animals, I get to contribute to work that is meaningful to me and has a huge impact. I've also learned some great skills that have helped me in my job hunting, too.

CHAPTER 17

LOOKING AFTER YOU

When you learn about what is happening to animals it can be overwhelming. You may feel sad, frustrated, and angry. If you see footage of animals being killed or living on factory farms, you will carry those memories with you. If you are at a vigil and look into the eyes of an individual who is about to be slaughtered, you may find yourself feeling broken inside.

It could be that you have been so busy juggling volunteering, petitions, protests, and schoolwork that you are feeling frazzled and burned out.

Burnout could even show as a physical symptom, such as lethargy.

Perhaps you feel guilty about your lack of action even though you are doing something to help animals.

It's essential to look after yourself. After all, you are an animal, too. How you feel is important. Many activists burn out after a short time of intense action. This is sad because it means the animals lose a skilled and powerful voice.

If activists don't look after themselves, they may experience symptoms such as depression, anxiety, and flashbacks.

I find that sometimes I get really sad after going to a factory farm. I may think of all the little faces I saw who are still in that awful place—all those little lives I was unable to help. I have to concentrate on the lives I have saved, as otherwise I would get overwhelmed and would find it hard to continue. I have to remember that every single life is important.

The activists in this book have been in a lot of difficult and stressful situations. They have found ways to keep going and look after themselves. Let's look at their experiences and see what tips we can take from them.

Zoe Rosenberg (15), San Luis Obispo, California

Every evening I try to read a book for thirty minutes before I go to bed. I think about something else for a little bit, and I can forget about all the suffering in the world.

I also find that having a community of like-minded people around me is helpful—people who also want to see a world where animals have rights. Whilst Facebook can be helpful, it can also be toxic, so finding an in-person community is perfect.

Jasmine Shaw (18), Central Coast, Australia

I struggled with burnout at first. When I first learnt what was happening to animals, I was so angry with everyone. I was yelling at my family, "How could you do this?" I was so upset. But then I began to use self-talk. I spoke to myself and said, "They aren't trying to annoy me. They just need help." If I want to stop animal abuse, I can't get hung up on my family. I have to focus that energy on people who are more willing to change. Sometimes I will use methods to distract myself for a bit, like going for a walk in nature.

Ateret Goldman (16), Berkeley, California

One thing that is important to avoid burnout is community. Another thing that helps me so much is sanctuaries. Sanctuaries are my home away from home wherever I am. Spending time with rescued animals rejuvenates me. I have had the pleasure of rescuing Hope the hen, and now I can go and visit her whenever I want. I have found out she is quite the troublemaker. She will flip over the food. She's not mean or a bully, but she's a troublemaker. Seeing where she was from and now seeing her as a little diva—it keeps me going. All the animals have a personality. It is just hidden behind the shield of exploitation.

Emi Pizarro Zamora (9), Brisbane, Australia

When I feel sad, I focus on the animals. I keep an image of them in my head. An image of them walking happy and free.

Kevin Courtney Black (22), California

To avoid burnout, try to make sure you have various external factors that help motivate you to keep you going. This could be your work or study. For example, when I am writing or acting I have to focus solely on that. It could be your friends, family, the desire for peace, the love for everyone, or a physical activity like yoga. Make sure you are taking breaks away from activism when needed. Please do not ignore your body. I find, once I get home from the protests, I either watch a movie or simply just give my friends a call and talk to them. Anything that gets my mind away from activism for a little bit.

Khendall Lil Bear (8), Florida

When I feel overwhelmed or angry, I think about how I will help animals and I think about how all this horrible stuff will be stopped one day.

Priscilla Huynh (20) Sydney, Australia

It is important to take the time to rejuvenate when you start to fatigue. Know the signs of burnout, such as if you find you lose patience when outreaching or if you are frequently feeling exhausted or sad after activism. When I am experiencing burnout or about to, I like to visit an animal sanctuary to witness animals that have been rescued and remember who I am fighting for. If you are unable to get to a sanctuary, you can read the stories of rescued animals on animal sanctuary social media pages and their websites. These stories give me hope and remind me to stay strong and continue speaking up for those whose voices are not heard.

Caylin King (17), Newcastle, Australia

I focus on the positive things that will happen. I think of the world going vegan. I know the suffering will end one day. It might not be now. I just want to do whatever I can to help animals until that happens. I find spending time with animals so soothing. I absolutely adore it. Their personalities are amusing and refreshing. I see the pigs and I watch them run. It makes me laugh. I look at them, and they just make me happy. They really help my mental health.

Emma Black (14), Wollongong, Australia

Sometimes I feel overwhelmed, especially if I am scrolling through social media and slaughterhouse footage comes up. I wonder how people can contribute to this and I feel sad. But then my mindset will change, and I'll be like, "What can I do to fix this?" and I'll come up with ideas and know I will make a difference. I can help change this. I also give myself time out and look after my mental health. I do yoga and meditation. I go to the beach and love to sing and play the guitar.

Oliver Davenport (17), Melbourne, Australia

Whilst photography is my main form of activism, I also use it as a way to avoid burnout. It gives me a break. I'll go to the park and take photos of nature and happy animals. I also give myself space between protests sometimes, just to take a breath.

BB (9), Chile

I do something to make me smile, like watch kitten videos on the internet or cuddle my cat.

Jacqueline (13), Ireland

I talk to vegan friends about how I feel. It helps to talk to someone who gets it.

Bailey Mason (16), Sydney, Australia

There are times when I feel sad and angry. I think you have to take a rest from time to time and look after yourself. It's important to look after yourself so you can look after the animals. Give yourself a break from the slaughterhouse footage, as it's heartbreaking. Take a rest. Get enough sleep. Don't feel like you have to do every single thing right now. Spend time with friends and family and people that you love.

Hannah McKay (16), Orange, New South Wales, Australia

I look at my companion animals and feel so thankful they are the species they are and that they are safe with me. They help me cope with the sad stuff. I make sure I do the best for my animal friends.

Vegan Evan (7), Florida

Spending time at farm sanctuaries makes me happy. I like to see animals safe and happy. I like pigs. They are very nice. I like to pat the pigs.

Charlotte Lim (22) of Sydney, Australia, knows how important it is to look after her mental health. She shared with me some of the ways she looks after herself. Maybe some of these ideas would work for you, too?

» If you can, spend time with animals. One of my favorite things about volunteering at NSW Hen Rescue is having unlimited access to the gorgeous animals at the headquarters. It's so uplifting seeing how happy and satisfied they are due to the collective effort of the vegan community. I love being able to have a lie in the sun with them.

» Spend as much time outdoors as possible, especially if you can't be around animals directly. Listen to birds in the trees and enjoy the noises of nature, as clichéd as it sounds. Buy some seed and feed street pigeons in parks.

» Talk to people. Talk to your friends who share the same passion as you. There is absolutely no shame in speaking to a psychologist to help deal and cope with burnout from activism. They're professionals, and they help.

» Eat some delicious vegan food. Cook something, or just buy yourself some delicious vegan junk food.

Haile Thomas (19), New York City

TO AVOID BURNOUT ...

» Take part in activities you enjoy, such as dancing, sports, hanging out with friends, spending time with happy animals, listening to music, or cooking.
» Give yourself at least thirty minutes before bed to relax and switch off. Read a fictional book or a magazine.
» Exercise regularly to get rid of stress.
» If it sounds appealing, you could try meditation or yoga as a calming way to start your day.
» Remind yourself of all the good you are doing.
» Take some time off if needed.
» Don't take on too much. Be okay with saying no.
» Get enough sleep.
» Surround yourself with people you love.
» Find a supportive animal rights community.
» Give yourself a break from social media.

Rescued hens hanging out with wild cockatoos at NSW Hen Rescue HQ

TO CHEER YOURSELF UP WHEN YOU ARE FEELING LOW ...

» Spend time in nature.
» Spend time with happy animals. Maybe take your dog for a long walk, sit with your companion chickens in the garden, watch the birds, or volunteer at a farm sanctuary.
» Take some deep, cleansing breaths and think of a vegan world and all the people who are working hard to make it happen.
» Exercise in whatever way feels fun for you. Maybe running, dancing, or kicking a ball around.
» Use positive self-talk: "I am doing all I can. Things will get better. There are lots of people who care."
» Watch something funny or entertaining.
» Try a creative outlet, such as journaling your feelings, writing a story, or creating some artwork.
» Call a vegan friend who gets it.
» Reach out to your local animal rights community and ask for support.
» If you feel depressed or are experiencing symptoms of PTSD, ask your parents if you can see a vegan counselor or make an appointment with an understanding doctor.
» Read the next chapter. There is hope.

CHAPTER 18

HOPE

When you are aware of all the horrible stuff that is going on in the world it can be overwhelming, but there is hope! Just take a look at this book and the unstoppable young activists featured. Think of what they will accomplish in the future. I find every one of them to be an incredible beacon of hope.

I bet you could be a changemaker, too. Maybe you will organize disruptions, rescues, or campaigns. Or perhaps you will make a difference with smaller actions. Imagine if everyone took small actions. It would create a much kinder world.

There are more vegans every day and more activists every day. There are also new technologies that will make being kind easier for people.

CULTIVATED MEAT

Sadly, there will always be some people who will not even consider going vegan. They may simply not care what animals go through, or they may be part of the industry and profit from animal suffering. As unlikely as it may seem, even those people may end up being kinder by accident.

New technologies are advancing that mean meat, eggs, dairy, and even leather and wool can be cultivated without slaughtering animals.

These products won't be "like" animal products. They will be exactly the same. The only difference is there is no slaughter involved. This is called *cultivated meat*, which has also been referred to as *cultured, cell-based,* or *clean meat.* Cultivated meat is made by growing cells in a nutrient serum. In theory, you only need one animal cell to start, and when it is placed in a nutrient serum, it will grow and multiply into muscle cells, which can then be formed into cultivated meat.

The goal is to make cultivated meat as cheap and widely available as meat from slaughtered animals. Although this sounds exciting, some animal activists are worried that cultivated meat has more negatives than positives.

Charlize Reynierse (22) of Sydney, Australia, says, "In my degree I have done a lot of cell culture. There are three ethical problems with it at the moment. The first is where you get the original animal cells from. This doesn't have to be an ethical problem, as cells could be gathered from an animal who has passed away from natural causes and then those cells could be replicated infinitely."

The second issue, she says, "is the serum we use to replicate the cells. This is fetal bovine serum, which is a product of cow slaughter. The reason this is used is because the serum contains growth factors that allow the cells to grow and replicate. It is used to develop many medicines and vaccines. I believe it is used because it works and it is cost effective and easy to obtain, but of course it has massive ethical problems. One way I can use my degree is to change the system from the inside and find a cost-effective, animal-free alternative to fetal bovine serum. I believe this is possible, and many cultivated meat companies are working on this, too."

Finally: "The third issue is that cell cultivation uses a lot of single-use plastics. This is another area that needs to be worked on. Despite this, cultivated meat is a lot better for the environment than meat from animal slaughter."

Charlize continues, "For me, I would not eat cultivated meat, as I get everything I need from plants and there seems like no need to have it available for humans. But I can see huge potential as far as pet food is concerned. If the price point could be lowered enough, carnivorous rescued animals like cats could eat a healthy diet without the need for the deaths of other animals. It would also be great for rescue centers that take in birds of prey, snakes, or other predators. Whilst I would not buy these products, they would be good for people who absolutely refuse to eat plant-based."

Charlize is right. As vegans, we may not be lining up to load up our trolleys with cultivated meat, but the potential to reduce animal suffering is immense, and with people like Charlize researching animal-free alternatives to fetal bovine serum and ways to reduce single-use plastics, imagine the animal lives that could be spared.

CAREER GOALS

Good at science? Food technology could be one major hope for animals. If you want to help animals, you could help develop slaughter-less meat. No animals involved!

PLANT-BASED MEAT

Every week it seems we have more plant-based sausages, burgers, and other meats available to us, and they seem to be getting yummier all the time. Sometimes it surprises me that more people are not already flocking to this stuff. It is delicious and so much healthier than animal flesh—plus there's no ick factor of eating a dead body. Perhaps it is the cost. At the moment a lot of veggie burgers are more expensive than meat. This will change!

Fast-food restaurants are adding cheap vegan burgers and pizzas to the menu. Plant-based meat doesn't come with the same ethical concerns as cultivated meat, and it is available right now. We are already beginning to see the downfall of dairy as plant-based milk becomes more popular, and there are even vegan eggs available.

Check out The Good Food Institute at GFI.org to learn more about cultivated meat and plant-based foods. If you want to make kind food your career, you will find plenty of useful info there to help you on your way.

CHOOSING A CAREER TO SAVE ANIMALS

There are so many career paths you can choose where you can help animals, whether working directly to save animals or being in a position of influence to help spread veganism and the message to be kind to animals.

Charlize Reynierse (22) of Sydney, Australia, chose her university course with the goal of helping animals.

> I always wanted to work with animals, even before I went vegan. I originally wanted to be a vet, but I didn't get the required grades, so I did animal science planning to transfer into a veterinary course later. In the end, I liked animal science. There are a lot of different things I can go into through animal science, and there are so many ways the degree helps me stand up for animals.
>
> My degree is called a Bachelor of Animal and Veterinary Bioscience. I major in animal health and disease. The degree teaches me a lot about the animal ag industry. It also gives me some authority to speak on the matter. Whilst that is not essential, it is helpful. It gives me the opportunity to choose subjects I want to research. I have an anonymous animal rights photography Facebook page. Sometimes I like to include scientific studies as references in my posts. For one assignment, I chose to write about gas chambers that they use to kill animals in some slaughterhouses. That gave me an excuse to look up lots of scientific articles on gas chambers. I learnt a lot about it and was able to include some of that research on my Facebook page.
>
> The other way the degree enables me to help animals is the career options. Whilst it feels like the degree is pushing students to work within animal agriculture, that is not what I will do. I want to be in a role where I can bring about real change for animals. At the moment, vaccines and medicines rely on animal products in their development and animal testing. I could take steps to make these processes vegan and develop non-animal alternatives.

My course has also helped me help animals through my placements. I have to do both farm and research placements for my degree. Seeing what happens to animals firsthand gives me more authority to speak on it. There is also the undercover aspect of university placement. I can gain access to witness what the animals are going through without the need to trespass or break any laws. If I film or take photographs as part of my course, I can use these to try and help future animals. It means I can be a whistleblower.

Whilst the course does give me opportunities to help animals, there have been a lot of challenges. It is so biased and tries to force you into the animal agriculture industry.

Every now and again, animal welfare will come up. It will be brushed off fairly quickly by the lecturers. They call vegans extremists, and it is infuriating. I majored in animal health and disease because I want to know about diseases in animals in the context of wanting to help animals, but I ended up learning about diseases in farm animals and what to do about them to make the most money. It did affect my performance in uni, as I couldn't justify listening in class anymore. Despite these challenges, I will be using my degree to help animals, and that is the most important thing.

CAREER IDEAS

There are ways to help animals and promote veganism in almost any job you can think of. Here are just a few ideas for careers in which you can help animals ...

Veterinarian

Vet nurse

Journalist

Photographer

Food tech scientist

Research scientist — non-animal methods

Chef

Author

Artist

Sanctuary owner or worker

Nonprofit worker

Vegan fashion designer

Vegan interior designer

Textile innovator

Documentary maker

Musician

Graphic designer for nonprofits

Undercover investigator

Plant-based nutritionist

Lawyer specializing in animal law

Politician

What's your dream job?

AS WE NEAR THE END OF THIS BOOK, I HOPE YOU ARE FEELING
INSPIRED AND EXCITED FOR THE FUTURE. REMEMBER TO USE THE
HASHTAG #SAVINGANIMALS SO I CAN SHARE YOUR GOOD WORK.

WHAT WILL THE WORLD BE LIKE FOR ANIMALS IN FIFTY YEARS?

Since we are ending this book with hope, let's sign off with a vision of the future as seen by young activists.

Vegan Evan (7), Florida

Everyone will recognize that what they are doing is hurting animals, and they will stop doing it. By then there will be so many vegans and activists. We will keep doubling the number of vegans again and again until everyone is vegan.

Bailey Mason (16), Sydney, Australia

I am absolutely confident that Dolphin Marine Magic will be no more and that the dolphins will be free. This won't happen in fifty years. This will happen very soon. There is a growing attitude that people just don't want to see ocean animals swimming around in tiny pools. With so many people speaking up against it, it will have to go. I will not stop until these dolphins are either free or moved to a sea sanctuary. I know the right thing for the dolphins will happen. A sea sanctuary or sea pen will be established. Seawater will be much better for dolphins than where they are kept now, in chlorinated pools. There will be no more aquariums and no more zoos or animal circuses. Only sanctuaries.

Priscilla Huynh (20) Sydney, Australia

I see the difference animal rights activism is making, and even if we can't change the direction the world is headed in, we can do our best to decrease the number of animals being born into the horrific agriculture industry. We can also rescue some of the animals who are currently being exploited. They need us to fight for them. If not you, then who?

Priscilla Huynh and Sydney the turkey

BB (9), Chile

I think things will be a lot better for animals. I believe that by then the Chilean rodeo will be shut down and there will be far less abandoned pets.

Khendall Lil Bear (8), Florida

Fifty years from now, the world will be so much better. I think most or all slaughterhouses will be gone.

Kevin Courtney Black (22), California

I think there will be more vegans and vegetarians, and the number of animals killed will go down dramatically. This will mean there will be far fewer animals raised into agriculture. Wild animals will also have an easier life as there will be less hunting.

Zoe Rosenberg (15), San Luis Obispo, California

Direct Action Everywhere has come up with a forty-year plan to ban meat and animal products in the U.S. I'm planning to help them achieve that. I want to build the animal rights movement that I promised Lero as I carried her from the slaughterhouse. One day we will have tens of thousands of people marching into slaughterhouses and taking the animals.

In fifty years, there will be a constitutional amendment for animal rights. In fifty years, we will have closed down most, if not all, slaughterhouses in the U.S. and will be tackling the ones operating illegally. Things can change so fast. I really believe that things will change for the animals. The people have the power to do whatever they set their minds to, no matter where they are, no matter who they are. We can bring about change.

Zoe rescuing hens from a caged egg farm

Ateret Goldman (16), Berkeley, California

In fifty years, these horrible farms that we fight so hard against will be turned into sanctuaries. These victims we see and cry for and whom we bear witness to will be living happy, healthy, and free. We will have mobilized so many people. We will have spoken up for those who have been silenced, and our collective voices will be so thunderous that they will no longer be ignored. Our world is going to be transformed. I believe we will have legal protection for animals. We're going to be living in a vegan world.

Ateret and fellow activists liberate baby lamb Edward from a slaughterhouse and take him to safety.

CONCLUSION

Thank you for reading this guide. Perhaps not everything in this book appeals to you, but I hope you will take something away and make it your own. For inspiration you might like to check out my fictional book about animal liberation, *Amanda the Teen Activist*, and search NSW Hen Rescue on Facebook, Instagram, or YouTube for the latest scoop from the coop.

Please know that you can and will make a difference if you put your mind to it. Your effort is worthwhile. Your voice is important. This situation is urgent, and no matter your physical ability, your race, your age, your culture, or your resources, there are ways for you to make a difference. If you need help, please reach out to me at catherinekelaher@gmail.com.

The thing I have taken away from writing this book and speaking to these amazing young activists is that there is so much hope. We will achieve change, and with you on board, it's going to happen faster than we ever thought possible. You are my hope. You are the animals' hope.

Love, Catherine x

Catherine and Maddie

FOR MORE INFORMATION

… on trawling: Carl Safina, "7 ways fishing trawlers are bad news for the seabed," Greenpeace.org/international/story/6895/7-ways-fishing-trawlers-are-bad-news-for-the-seabed

… on long lines: PETA.org/issues/animals-used-for-food/factory-farming/fish/commercial-fishing

… on bycatch: ""Why Wild-Caught Shrimp Aren't as Innocent as You Think," Medium.com/sustainable-seafood/why-wild-caught-shrimp-arent-as-innocent-as-you-think-974e9053638c

…on Inky the octopus: "The great escape: Inky the octopus legs it to freedom from aquarium," TheGuardian.com/world/2016/apr/13/the-great-escape-inky-the-octopus-legs-it-to-freedom-from-new-zealand-aquarium

… on downed animals: "Downed Cow: The True Story of One Anonymous Animal Born Into the Meat Industry," PETA.org/features/downed-cow-meat-industry

… on leather: "Environmental Hazards of Leather," PETA.org/issues/animals-used-for-clothing/leather-industry/leather-environmental-hazards

… on animal research in the U.S.: AAVS.org/animals-science/animals-used

… on animal research in Australia: AnimalsAustralia.org/issues/animal_experimentation.php

… on protein in spinach: Healthyeating.sfgate.com/much-protein-spinach-5826.html

… on iron: Ncbi.nlm.nih.gov/pmc/articles/PMC3685880

… on osteoporosis and cow's milk: FoodMatters.com/article/the-truth-about-calcium-and-osteoporosis

… on fishes and memory: "Three-second memory myth: Fish show they can remember things for up to five months," DailyMail.co.uk/sciencetech/article-1106884/Three-second-memory-myth-Fish-remember-months.html

… on lost dogs in storms: "Lost dog numbers triple after storms," ABC.net.au/news/2010-03-11/lost-dog-numbers-triple-after-storms/359630

… on human overpopulation: Assets.prb.org/pdf10/10wpds_eng.pdf

… on deforestation: Cowspiracy.com/facts

… on kangaroo killing: KangarooTheMovie.com and AnimalAaustralia.org/issues/kangaroo_shooting.php

… on ocean plastic pollution: "The Great Pacific Garbage Patch Isn't What You Think it Is," NationalGeographic.com/news/2018/03/great-pacific-garbage-patch-plastics-environment/

… on cultivated meats: "This startup is making real meatballs in a lab without killing a single animal," BusinessInsider.com.au/memphis-meats-lab-grown-meatballs-2016-11

… on the downfall of dairy: FoodRevolution.org/blog/problems-with-dairy

ACKNOWLEDGMENTS

This book would not have been possible without the young activists who are changing the world. They volunteered their time so I could chat with them about their work, and they put themselves out there every day to be a force of good for the animals. Thank you, Emma Black, Jacqueline, Oliver Davenport, Emi Pizarro Zamora, Hannah McKay, Katie Lynch-Dombroski, Bailey Mason, Haile Thomas, Hannah Testa, Ateret Goldman, Caylin King, Jasmine Shaw, Gemma Krogh, Morgan Greenfield, Danielle Greenfield, Jack Upperton, Summer Upperton, Grace Upperton, Khendall Lil Bear, Vegan Evan, Zoe Rosenberg, BB, Charlize Reynierse, Priscilla Huynh, Kevin Black, Charlotte Lim, Callan Flynn, and Kenia and Bianca Jade Bizzocchi—and a throwback thank you to my school BFF Melissa, who was by my side right at the beginning.

A huge thank you to Jess Henderson for the beautiful art.

Thank you to the activists who put valuable time aside to help proofread this book. You were all amazing.

David Kelaher, Sarah Morrison, and Ana Lopes, thank you for your friendship, support, ideas, and help with editing. You give me endless hope.

And thank you to all my activist friends and those activists I have not yet met. I know you are all working so hard to create a vegan world.

KEEP GOING. WE ARE GETTING THERE.

Artwork by Jessica Henderson

ABOUT THE AUTHOR

Catherine Kelaher is the founder of NSW Hen Rescue, an Australian charity that rescues, rehabilitates, and rehomes hens and other animals from factory farms. Both Catherine and NSW Hen Rescue have received awards for animal activism and rescue.

Catherine was born and raised in England and studied English literature and creative writing at Kingston Upon Thames University. She moved to Sydney in 2006 and has been rescuing animals and trying to make the world a better place ever since.

ABOUT THE PUBLISHER

Ashland Creek Press is an independent, vegan-owned publisher of environmental literature, which includes books in all genres about animals, the environment, and the planet we all call home. We are passionate about books that foster an appreciation for worlds outside our own, for nature and the animal kingdom, and for the ways in which we all connect. To learn more, visit us at www.AshlandCreekPress.com.

8/22 - 0

CPSIA information can be obtained
at www.ICGtesting.com
Printed in the USA
BVHW040820040521
606411BV00011B/136

9 781618 220943